P. E. Gordon

50 SERMON–TALKS
FOR BOYS AND GIRLS

50 SERMON–TALKS
FOR BOYS AND GIRLS

By

CARL S. WEIST

WILLETT, CLARK & COMPANY

CHICAGO   NEW YORK

1936

To

BARBARA ANN AND CARL FREDERICK

WHO IN EARLY CHILDHOOD HAVE GIVEN

THEIR FATHER MANY SERMON TALKS

FOREWORD

THESE TALKS ARE written for boys and girls from seven to thirteen years of age. Consequently some of them, for example, " An Animal Track Meet," may seem very childish to juniors nearing the teen age. On the other hand, other talks draw from experiences which are as yet alien to the younger child. The reader will grade as he reads, endeavoring always to keep in mind that few are intended for all ages.

A serious attempt has been made to avoid themes which are peculiar to and of especial delight to adults. The writer is always suspicious of a sermon to children when it is too cordially received by older people, as it very possibly means that the lesson is far over the minds of younger folk. Talking to adults in the congregation over the heads of boys and girls is always a temptation and always disastrous from the standpoint of benefiting the child. To confine the themes to a child's experiences narrows the range and makes for some repetition but renders the lessons understandable and serviceable — partly, perhaps, because of the repetition.

As far as possible the language of the original talks has been retained. This accounts for the informal, chatty atmosphere which permeates many of them.

That the reader may catch some of the joy which the writer had when looking into the radiant faces of boys and girls from Sunday to Sunday, and may find stimulus for far better talks than these, this book is hopefully presented.

CARL S. WEIST

CONTENTS

50 SERMON–TALKS
FOR BOYS AND GIRLS

And he called to him a little child, and set him in the midst of them, and said, Verily I say unto you, except ye turn, and become as little children, ye shall in no wise enter into the kingdom of heaven. — MATTHEW 18:2, 3

" The time has come," the Walrus said,
  " To talk of many things:
Of shoes — and ships — and sealing-wax —
  Of cabbages — and kings —
And why the sea is boiling hot —
  And whether pigs have wings."
— LEWIS CARROLL

CALAMITY JANE

He that is slow to anger is better than the mighty;
And he that ruleth his spirit, than he that taketh
a city. PROVERBS 16:32

LET US SAY IT this way: the boy who keeps from getting angry is stronger than a boy with big bones and hard muscles. The girl who is able to control her temper and keep sweet is stronger than a soldier who captures a city. The boy or girl who learns to be calm and gentle is fairly sure to win out in life over those who fly into rages all the time.

Some years ago there was a boy who used to go to the golf links with his father. He would take a club or two and practice swinging. Soon he was beating his own dad, but his father did not mind that because he noticed that his son played like a real golfer.

As years went on, the boy played better and better. Some days he played like a champion. As long as everything went well he could play well, but let him have a little hard luck — let his ball roll into a hole on the fairway, back of a tree, or into a " bad lie " — and he would grow angry, particularly if he made several bad shots in getting his ball out of these hard places. He would stamp about, throw his club away, or break it up.

This went on for several years. Everyone said he would be a great player if it were not for this weakness. One day he realized this and said to himself: " I must learn to control my temper." It was a long, hard fight, but he won.

1

This is the interesting fact: just as soon as he learned to control his temper, he learned to control his golf shots. He became the greatest golf player the world has ever known, the pride of the South and of all America. Who? Bobby Jones, of course, Robert T. Jones, to be exact. In 1930 he won the amateur championship and the open championship of England, and the same two cups in America.

What made him so great? His knack of hitting the ball just right? His years of constant practice? Yes, they helped. But I think the greatest element in his golf greatness was the fact that he learned to rule his spirit.

He was as calm and unruffled in a match as anyone could be. At Columbus, Ohio, during the National Open Golf Tournament, I saw one of his shots from the tee bound down a hill into grass a foot high, just back of a stony brook. There were trees between him and the green. Remember, he won by only one shot. I saw him calmly walk down, take a club, then standing knee-deep in the grass, swing firmly. The ball leaped out of the grass, sailed over the trees, and stopped fifteen feet from the cup on the green. He took his favorite putter, " Calamity Jane," and sank the ball for a three.

There is a lesson for you and me here. We want to be strong — no one wants to be a weakling — but we do not know how. We think we will impress our parents or playmates if we become angry, snap them off with our words and go sweeping about, having our own sweet or ugly way.

" That doesn't work," says Bobby Jones. " That doesn't work," says the proverb writer. " If you wish to become really strong, learn to control your temper. Keep cool, if you would win."

2

ALIBI IKE

Ye were running well; who hindered ye?
GALATIANS 5:7

PAUL WROTE THIS in a letter to the people of Galatia. Some time before he must have seen them racing. Suddenly some of them fell behind and dropped out of the race. Paul, looking on, must have said to himself: " What's the trouble? You were doing well. What happened? "

We do not have their answers, but I would bet that they were like these:

One of the runners: " I couldn't run as well as usual because my shoe-lace became untied."

Another: " I stopped because a pebble got into my shoe."

Another: " I slipped just as I was going around the corner. If I had not slipped I would have won."

Another: " I did not have time to train and so I lost my breath too soon."

Another: " I have to work too hard, and I was tired before I began. The one who won doesn't have to work as hard as I do."

Another: " That fellow has run so much longer than I have. No wonder he won."

Can you imagine them writing these things to Paul? Do you suppose he believed them? No, I do not believe he did. He probably knew at once that they were alibis or excuses. Instead of saying: " The runner who came out ahead was better than I," " He was too fast for me,"

3

or " I ran as well as I ever do, but he beat me fairly," they made themselves ridiculous with their excuses. Do you know what we call people like that? Alibi Ikes.

What is an Alibi Ike? He is one who is always making excuses for himself. If he loses a game, it is never his fault. Something always happens. He is never willing to admit that others can do anything better than he can.

When I was your age, in a small country, red-brick schoolhouse, we had our picture taken. When the proofs came and we were looking at them — trying to find ourselves, of course — one boy said, " I would have been the best looking, if I hadn't had sore eyes." The picture was so small that we could not see the eyes at all, but that was his alibi just the same for his funny face.

Did you ever see an Alibi Ike in school? He is always blaming something for his lack of preparation. He says, " I had too much to do last evening; I didn't have time to get my lessons "; " My eyes hurt and I couldn't study "; or something like that. He neglects to say that the fault was really his; he did not " choose " to study.

There are Alibi Ike girls also. They say, " I could do thus and so, too, if I had the chance that girl has. See what nice clothes she has, and what a lot of money, and such a large house. No wonder she is so smart. She hasn't anything to do at home and everything is given to her." Did you ever hear anything like that? Well, when you hear it, just put it down as another Alibi Ike. For we know that when you and I really set out with all our hearts to do something, no small thing will stand in the way. We have the same chance as others have, if only we think we have.

Alibi Ike makes me think of some of our football teams. A few days before a football game we read re-

4

ports of certain teams, Yale, Princeton, Harvard, Army, and we feel so badly for them. The writer says that they are all crippled up. The article sounds as though the men would not be able even to walk on the fields, let alone run. One expects to see the whole team come out on crutches. Instead, on the day of the game out comes a team of healthy looking young men. Why the stories, then? You see, it was Alibi Ike working. He was preparing us for his team to be beaten so that he could say afterward: " We did not play as well as usual. Three of our players were crippled. If we had had our full strength, etc, etc."

I am saying all this because I want you to play hard and fairly. Work as hard as you can; use all the brains you have; run as fast as ever you can, and if you are beaten, do not blame anyone else. Admit defeat and say: " It was my own fault. I played the best I could, but you played better than I did. Perhaps the next time I'll do better." Hit the line as hard as you can, and do not whine when you are thrown back. Don't be an Alibi Ike.

ROOSEVELT — THE GENTLEMAN

And the servant of the Lord must be gentle to-
wards all.   II TIMOTHY 2:24

" HE IS A GENTLEMAN," I heard a man say of another a
short time ago. What did he mean? When we speak of
a gentleman, what kind of a person are we referring to?

I will tell you what an old colored man thinks a gentleman is. This story by Orland K. Armstrong appeared
in the *New York Herald Tribune* not long ago. Uncle
Holt Collier lives at Greenville, Mississippi. Uncle
Holt is the best bear hunter in that country; indeed he
is so good that when President Theodore Roosevelt
wanted to go bear hunting, who but Uncle Holt was
asked to be the guide.

" Sho' I was a bear hunter! Reckon I was de best shot
erroun' hyar! " says Uncle Holt.

He still has the high-powered bear gun the President
gave him because of his skill and marksmanship. And
when anyone approaches him Uncle Holt is sure to produce the gun and tell some stories of how he hunted
with the President.

One story particularly he enjoys telling. They were
out one day when Uncle Holt's two lead dogs found the
trail. Away they went barking, for they were so well-
trained that they would bark at nothing but a bear. Mr.
Roosevelt had asked why he had named one of the
dogs " Boston." " That dog doesn't look like Boston,"
the President commented. " He reminds me more of
Cheyenne."

6

"By an' by," says Uncle Holt, in telling of the incident, "Lucy and Boston open up, and I know dey gettin' close. I could tell de minute dey found dat bear, and by de yelps I knew he weighed about six hundred pounds. Sho' 'nough, when I get to de spot whar de dogs worryin' him, he's er big gray bear weighin' 'bout six hundred pounds."

The bear fought for several hours. He charged at the dogs who sniffed at him, always gliding out of reach in time to escape. At last, says Holt, the bear took up his position by the side of a rock. Here he stood at bay. Uncle Holt called off the dogs. Making ready a rope, with his knife and rifle at hand, he advanced cautiously, and when within a few feet he called to a dog, "Ketch him, Jocko!" The dog sprang at the bear's hind legs, and as the bear turned to spring at Jocko, Uncle Holt slipped the lariat noose over bruin's neck and forepaws. Then he led the bear back to the camp.

"Bully for you! I knew you would do it!" roared the President. (It seems there had been a discussion as to whether a bear could be lassoed).

"Shoot the bear! Shoot him, Colonel!" shouted some of the men.

At this, Uncle Holt says, Colonel Roosevelt turned on the men and snapped through his teeth: "What sort of sport would that be?" Then he explained to the shame-faced group, the old hunter tells us, that he would never take an unsportsmanlike advantage of a beast.

"He was er gentleman, dat's what he was," Uncle Holt adds. "He was kind, an' friendly, an' interested in everybody, an' erfraid o' nothin'. Ain't that er gentleman? Yas, suh!"

I think we would agree with Uncle Holt that it is. Here are his four points:

A gentleman is kind. Kind to animals, kind to brothers and sisters, kind to everyone and everything. Gentle. Timothy says in our text that this is one way of telling whether we are Christians. " A servant of God," he writes, " must be gentle towards all." According to this, no rough, harsh, unkind person can be considered a *gentle-man*. Again, a gentleman, according to Uncle Holt, is friendly. Third, a gentleman is interested in everybody. A gentleman cannot be a snob, going along with his head up in the air, high-hatting everyone. He must be interested in everyone. If we are interested in people, we shall sympathize and want to help them. George Bernard Shaw, on being asked to tell what he thought a gentleman is, said: " A gentleman is one who tries to put back a little more than he takes out." Uncle Holt's fourth point is this: " A gentleman is erfraid of nothin'! " That is, he must have courage. So here we have it — what is a gentleman? He is a man who is kind, friendly, unselfish and courageous.

" Ain't that er gentleman? Yas, suh! "

RUNNING TOWARD YOUR OWN GOAL

*Then Judas, who betrayed Jesus, when he saw
that Jesus was condemned, repented himself,
and brought back the thirty pieces of silver to
the chief priests and elders. . . . And he went
away and hanged himself.*　MATTHEW 27:3, 5

THAT WAS A VERY sad death.　Here was Judas, one of the
disciples, who walked and talked with Jesus for several
years.　He had every chance to become honest and
noble, but he threw his chances away and betrayed Jesus
with a kiss.　It was Judas, you remember, who in the
Garden of Gethsemane kissed Jesus and in so doing told
the Roman soldiers who Jesus was.　Realizing what he
had done, Judas went away and took his own life.

In other words he ran toward the wrong goal.　He defeated himself; no one was responsible for his failure
but himself.

We shall never forget a football player who defeated
himself.　Perhaps you listened on the radio to the game
that was played in California between the University of
California and Georgia Tech one New Year's Day.　If
you did, you will remember this.　When the California
team was within twenty-five yards of Georgia Tech's
goal-line, the ball was fumbled and Riegels of California
recovered it.　Instead of running with it toward Tech's
goal, however, he somehow became confused, and wheel-
ing about ran seventy-five yards toward his own goal
with his own team-mates close at his heels, begging him
to stop.　He did come to his senses within a foot of his

own goal but the kick-out by his own team-mates was blocked and Georgia Tech scored a safety — two points — enough to win the game. Riegels was his own worst enemy, was he not? He defeated himself.

Some of you perhaps have read the books, *Meet General Grant* and *John Brown's Body*, which tell the story of the Civil War in our country, 1861 to 1865. You will recall that the two generals whom the southern soldiers loved and revered were Stonewall Jackson and Robert E. Lee. At the Battle of the Wilderness, Stonewall Jackson was riding back toward his own lines when he was fired upon by a company of southern soldiers. He was mortally wounded, killed by his own men who would gladly have given their lives for him. They were their own worst enemies. In other words, they ran toward the wrong goal. They defeated themselves.

Now, perhaps we will understand what Theodore Roosevelt meant when he said: "A nation's worst foes are those of its own household." Judas' worst enemy was himself. Riegels' worst enemy was not Georgia Tech, but himself. The southern soldiers' worst enemies were themselves. All these defeated themselves. Do you see?

And I wonder whether it is true sometimes of boys and girls. We run toward the wrong goal. We defeat ourselves.

Here is a boy who goes out on a rainy or snowy day and gets his shoes and stockings wet. He knows what he should do, but he does not do it. Instead, he keeps on playing, and the first thing he knows, he has to take a large tablespoonful of a certain kind of liquid he does not relish and is put to bed for several days. Not always, but usually, we run toward the wrong goal and bring colds and grippe on ourselves. We defeat our own health by carelessness and neglect.

Again, here is a girl who is lonely. She has no friends. No one seems to want to play with her. Do you know why? Well, I do not know exactly, of course, but I can guess fairly well. If I were betting, I would wager a large amount that this particular girl is mean to other girls, extremely selfish, wanting everything for herself, or thinks herself a little above everyone else. The fault of her friendlessness lies within herself and not with others, for all of these things I have mentioned she could cure. No one compels her to be cross, ugly or selfish. She allows herself to get that way and when she does so, no one wants to be near her. She defeats herself. She runs toward the wrong goal.

AN ANIMAL TRACK MEET

ONCE UPON A TIME some animals were holding a track meet. It was a warm spring day and clover was in bloom. They had come to the third event of the afternoon: Peter Rabbit was to race Ebenezer Turtle. Everything was arranged. Dicky Squirrel sat on the stake. Bob White was to whistle and clear the track. Billy Goat was to be judge at the finish because he could signal with his tail to the assembled spectators when the winner seized the tape. Johnny Skunk was the starter. The committee selected him because they thought the runners would be more anxious to get away. Percy Porcupine was to do the scoring with his quill pens.

So they lined them up and Bob White sang out in his usual manner: " On your marks! Get set! Go! "

Away they went, Peter Rabbit hippety-hoppety-ing, hippety-hoppety-ing until he was lost to sight over a hill; Ebenezer Turtle shuffling along as fast as he could. There was no danger of Ebenezer's burning up the cinder path.

Pretty soon Peter looked around and there was nobody in sight. He sniffed. " Clover! Delicious, sweet clover! I haven't had any today. (He hadn't wanted to eat before the races.) Ebenezer isn't in sight. I'll just go over into Farmer Brown's field and have a little breakfast." So he went over and ate and ate and ate, till he could eat no more, and before he knew it, he fell fast asleep.

In the meantime Billy Goat, the judge of the race, grew very tired of waiting, and being hungry, too, ate

12

three tin cans before his hunger was satisfied. Then he lay down and before he knew it, he too was fast asleep.

But Ebenezer kept shuffling and shuffling until late in the afternoon. He was very near the line when Peter suddenly awoke and rubbed his eyes. " My goodness," he exclaimed, " what was I doing? Oh yes, I was racing." And away he went through the fence and down the road.

But he was too late. Ebenezer seized the tape just an instant before Peter arrived. And what excitement there was! All the animals danced and flew around shouting, " Hoora! Hoora! for Ebenezer! " Then they all gathered about while beautiful Miss Nanny Goat presented Ebenezer with a little Ford roadster, starter and everything.

You see, Peter was a very good beginner but a mighty poor finisher. Did you ever hear of the man who built a house and never put a roof on it? He sat fiddling in front of his house one day, when a traveler asked, " Stranger, why don't you put a roof on your house? " " When it rains I can't and when it doesn't rain I don't need any," he answered.

He is very like a boy who begins his homework, but hearing a whistle in the midst of his work, immediately drops what he is doing to join the marble game.

Over a certain tailor shop there was this sign, " Finishers wanted." True! That is what the world wants. The world wants boys and girls who will finish what they begin. Our Master wants that kind in his Kingdom. The kingdom of love will never be built by folks who make a start at it and then go to eating clover blossoms.

13

THE MAN WHO SAWED OFF THE LIMB

So are the ways of every one that is greedy of
gain; it taketh away the life of the owners thereof.

PROVERBS 1:19

THAT IS TO SAY, a greedy boy and girl take away their
own happiness. They spoil their own lives. For greed
is selfishness; selfishness makes us unhappy; unhappiness
robs our lives.

A few weeks ago I heard of a man who wanted to saw
off a limb from a tree. He climbed out on the limb and,
placing the saw between himself and the trunk of the
tree, began sawing. When the limb was sawed off he fell
to the ground with it and was crippled for life. He had
sawed off the limb on which he was sitting.

He makes me think of the man who was out in a boat.
He started to bore a hole in the bottom of the boat under
the board on which he was seated. Others in the boat
protested. " Why worry? " he said, " I'm only boring a
hole under my own seat." He was sawing off the limb
on which they were sitting.

Many years ago Rome was a strong nation. Across
the Mediterranean Sea was Carthage, also a strong and
wealthy nation. Rome did not like Carthage. She was
jealous of her. So one day Rome went over and killed
the people, destroyed the city, and sowed with salt the
ground where the city had stood.

What was the result? Rome found her own ships
lying idle in the harbors. Carthage had bought goods
from Rome and had shipped her goods to Rome. Rome,

14

in destroying Carthage, had killed her best customer. In destroying Carthage, Rome had slain her best friend. Do you see how Rome sawed off the limb on which she had been sitting?

Do boys and girls ever do that? Do they sink their own boats? I think so. Occasionally you hear of a girl "putting on airs," "trying to be high-hat" or "stuck-up." She refuses to speak to someone or acts very proud. The one who does that thinks she is making herself very important in the eyes of others. She thinks she is making an "imprint," as Andy says. She says to herself: "When Susie sees me coming down the street she will be very jealous. I'll bet she would love to be like me."

I do not know how you feel about it, but it strikes me that girl is sawing off the limb on which she is sitting. For pretty soon with a jolt she comes down to earth. She finds she has lost most of her friends. There is an old saying, "He that spits against the wind spits in his own face." That is what "up-stage," "stuck-up" boys or girls do. They make everyone dislike them. No one wants "high-hat" persons for his friends. Usually they are not good friends.

Let us take another case. I think a boy saws off the limb on which he is sitting when he spends his money carelessly or too easily. You know there are boys who think that all money is for is to spend, to have a good time with. As soon as they get it they spend it, often for something too soon eaten up or broken.

That is one reason so many people die poor. When they were boys and girls like you they never learned how to be thrifty. There is a Scout Law which reads, "A Scout is thrifty." We are told that only five out of one hundred men and women when they become sixty-five years of age have saved enough to keep themselves comfortably the remaining years of their lives. It is so easy to get the habit of spending, so easy to become a spendthrift, and it is so difficult to break the habit. The spendthrift thinks he will always have money to spend. He keeps on sawing, sitting on the limb; when it suddenly drops and his money runs out, it is often too late in life to earn more. Then, too, when there are so many in the world who need physicians, hospitals, schools, clothes and food, it is a pity if we spend too much foolishly upon ourselves.

Again, I think boys and girls saw off the limb on which they are sitting if each day they do not do their very best in school. I know boys who think they are being very smart if they succeed in making their teachers believe they have their work done when they do not have it. After a time they fall into slip-shod habits of study, and later on when they really wish to study, they find they do not know how. They are not laying a sure foundation.

Some day they must go out from home to earn their living. Many boys and girls have had to go to night school because they did not do thoroughly each day's work as it came along. And many have never done what they should have done in life because they were not properly prepared for the task assigned them in business or profession.

Remember this then: when you trim your trees of life, be sure you are not sitting out on the limb.

TELEVOX — VOICE FROM AFAR

He that loveth not knoweth not God; for God
is love.   I JOHN 4:8

I WONDER WHETHER you have ever heard of a Televox. The name comes from a Greek word and a Latin word which when placed together mean, " Voice from afar." A Televox is an electrical man. Its vital organs are very funny. Instead of heart, lungs, stomach, it has switches, coils, transformers, vacuum tubes, electrical devices of all kinds. This man absolutely obeys his master's voice. He can do only certain things, but he does those very well. There are two of his family now in use in Washington, D. C. They tell the central station how high the water is in the reservoir. Wires could be run to the substation but that would be expensive, so the telephone already there is utilized. The man at the central station speaks to the Televoxes over the phone with tuning forks and they do what is wanted, so long as the wants are not too great. They have not much in the way of a voice, but they can make noises, buzzes and funny sounds. The inventor, R. J. Wensley, has one in his laboratory which will open a safe door when he says, " Open sesame." The Televox understands the words, at least well enough to open a door.

The inventor says that very soon we shall have these weird men in our houses, answering the phone, turning off or on the draft of the furnace, turning on or off the pianola or radio, lighting the lights, putting out milk bottles, and doing goodness knows what else. How

17

would you like to have one of these Televoxes working in your house?

When I heard of this Televox I thought to myself, what is the difference between a Televox and boys and girls? A Televox has ears, eyes, a body, arms and voice. He can do some things. So far he is much like you.

No further than that however does the likeness go. For the Televox is a machine. He can do only certain things; you can do many things. He cannot think. If gas were filling a room, he would strike a match just the same, and blow up the house. A Televox cannot feel. No matter who is ill in the house he would not care a bit. It would not make any difference to him if boys and girls were starving on the front step of the house; he would turn on the radio just the same.

As I thought more about it, however, and remembered about some boys and girls I have known, I decided that there are some like these Televoxes. I have named them Televox-boys and Televox-girls. They do not think much. They do not use their heads. They are like machines. They do things in a certain way because they did things that way before.

A member of this class told me a story about a boy who did not use " the sense he was born with." One day he came home carrying a dog. His mother said, " You should lead him with a leash." The next day he came home dragging a loaf of bread by a leash. His mother made some pies. " Now be careful," she said, " how you step in these pies." When he came home, the boy carefully stepped in the center of each pie. " My mother said I should be careful how I stepped in these pies," he told his friend. He was a Televox-boy, a sort of machine without a mind.

Some girls do things without thinking because some

other girls do them. If other girls have many dresses, they think they should have as many. They do not stop to think whether the dresses are absolutely necessary or whether their parents can afford them. The Televox-girl says: "Sally Juniper is going tonight. I'm going too." Do you know what a mob is? It is a group of people who lose their heads, tear down buildings and hang other men. They are all Televoxes. They do not think about what they are doing at all; they have lost the use of their minds.

But you need not smile. Boys are Televoxes when they are thoughtless. They do not think of ways of helping mother around the house. They leave things for mother to pick up. They clutter up the house with their books and playthings.

Then there is another kind of Televox-boy and girl. They are the ones who do not have much feeling for others. They go stamping about the house or church like electric men, machines trampling on the rights of others. They say bitter, sharp things, forgetting that folks are not Televoxes, but have feelings. They never see that others may be less fortunate than they and might be helped by a cheerful word or a smile.

Two girls come to church school. Both hear of a way of doing something at Christmas for someone else. The one pays no attention and straightway forgets; the other feels sorry, remembers, and brings some article the next Sunday that will help to give someone a merry Christmas. Which is a girl; and which is a Televox? Think that over and answer it at Christmas time.

A GOOD SPORT

For though the fig tree shall not flourish, neither shall fruit be in the vines; yet I will rejoice in God.   HABAKKUK 3:17, 18

WHEN I READ this verse in which Habakkuk in spite of all his losses and failures rejoices in the good things he has left, I think that the old prophet must have been a good sport.

Do you know what a good sport is? We hear that phrase quite often. " He is a good sport " or " She is a good sport." What do we mean by good sportsman-ship?

Some years ago a cup was presented by Mayor Walker to the " Best Loser " in the world, and perhaps the best sport in the world. Sir Thomas Lipton who received it was from England and every ten years he built a sail boat to compete with America's best boat. In all his at-tempts he never won the race. Each time he smiled and said, " We'll try again." Each time he built another " Shamrock " which lost. It was the dream of his life to take the cup back to England but he was never able to do it.

Now why did the whole world love this man and make so much of him? Why was a cup, paid for by contribu-tions from his American admirers, presented to him to compensate for the loss of the championship cup? Why? Because he knew how to lose. He never whined or kicked, nor said slurring things about the boat that beat him. He always smiled and pointed out why the boat was better than his. He took his defeat medicine so easily that it actually made him victorious. In other words, he was a winner even when he lost.

There are some people who do not know how to lose. If their football team loses a game once a season they whine, grumble, and say slighting things about the coach and the school authorities. They are poor sports, I think, who have never learned how to take defeat.

Everyone cannot win all the time; somebody must lose. It is no disgrace to lose if we play as clean and hard as we can. The disgrace comes afterward in the things we say about the winning team or about our hard luck. Some teams, some boys, never lose a football game without talking about breaks. The other team had all the breaks, that is, they had all the luck. Sometimes it is true, but a loser should never talk about it. The old prophet said, " If there are no grapes in my vineyard and no cattle in my stable, and someone else gets all the breaks, I am still going to rejoice. Never mind what happens, I will face it cheerfully."

Harvard unexpectedly beat Yale in November, 1930, at New Haven. It was almost what the sport-writers call an upset. I was interested in what a writer said the next day. He wandered about the Yale campus after the defeat, but he heard not one word except praise for the Harvard team. Yale did not say, " Harvard cheated. Harvard played a rough game. Harvard had all the breaks." They said, " We lost fairly to a good team, and now we must wait till next year." That is what I mean by good sportsmanship.

But there is such a thing as being a good sport when you win. Have you ever seen a boy very cocky after winning a game, so strutty that the loser is made to feel badly? Let me tell you about a sportsmanlike winner.

Several years ago Johnny Doeg defeated Richard Shields at Forest Hills for the tennis championship of America. It was a hard match and either might have won at several points in the play. Finally Johnny Doeg won and was escorted to the microphone to speak over the radio. What did he say? " This is the proudest moment of my life, to win this cup for dear old California "? No. He said instead, " Shields played a great game. I was mighty lucky to win."

So you and I must learn how to lose and how to win in this life. It is not only in games that we lose. Sometimes perhaps you fail in your school work. What do you say: " It was the teacher's fault. He should have kept me from failing "? I hear that sometimes and smile. I know it may be the teacher's fault now and then, but usually I know whose fault it is. A good sport after failure says: " It was my fault. I did not work hard enough. I loafed when I should have been studying. Give me another chance. I'll show you I can do better."

You and I are always trying to make excuses for ourselves, are we not? Instead of saying, " It is wrong. I know I should not get angry so easily; I shall try to stop flying into a rage over nothing," we blame it on someone else. We say: " It was brother's fault. He shouldn't have teased the cat. He shouldn't have taken my ball. I would have been all right if he had left me alone." A good sport takes the blame when it is his, and sometimes when it is not.

Let us try to be good sports whether we win or lose.

THE SCRUB TEAM

*But many shall be last that are first; and first that
are last.* MATTHEW 19:30

Do you know what a scrub team is? It is not what some
of you may be thinking: a team that scrubs floors. It is
a team of football players who are not quite good enough
to make the second or first teams. Because they do not
make these first teams we never hear the names of these
scrub players. They are never mentioned in the All-
American team. On the day of the game when the first
team warms up and the rooters cheer for them, shouting
their names, the scrub team sits on the side-lines un-
noticed. There are no cheers for them.

And yet I sometimes think that the scrub team is more
important than the first team. This is why I think it.
The scrub team comes out to practice every day and
often plays the first team. The first team practices on
them; runs through and over them, tackles them, blocks
them out, knocks them over, but the scrubs play on just
the same. For what? Well, to make the first team
strong. They do all the hard, grinding work in order
that these first team men will win their games on Satur-
days. Before a big game the scrubs learn the plays of
the visiting team and try them on the first team. Without the scrub teams the first teams would never be what
they are. I think that is what Jesus meant when he
said, " The last shall be first." " The scrubs shall be
first."

You see now why the " scrubs," as they are unjustly

called, deserve so much praise. Without a chance for fame, without praise or mention, they plug along with their hard work for the sake of others in their college or high school. I think they are heroes in a way, because it takes more courage for a scrub player to keep going than it does a first team player. At Princeton University, I am told, there is a plate in honor of the scrub teams who work so loyally for their college.

Some time ago I read of a " scrub " at Ohio State University. For four years he had gone out day after day to help the first team, never missing a practice. All that time he had never had a chance to play in a game. In the last game of his senior year, however, the coach sent him in to play for several minutes. It was a fine thing for the coach to do, was it not? The player knew at last that his work had been worth something and that he was good enough to play at least a few minutes with the varsity. " He was a hero," said the writer, though he probably called himself a " scrub."

There are a good many folks in this world who are heroes though they never become known to you and to me. They never have solo parts in the orchestra. They always help someone else, but what a large part they do play! You see the minister and the choir on Sunday morning, for example, and seldom see the sexton of the church. But did you ever stop to think why it is warm for you on Sunday mornings? It is because our sexton gets up very early and comes here while you are sleeping, to start the fire. You may not think he is so important, but just let him miss sometime and see how you would feel. A sexton on a zero morning is a hero.

Or take the men who bring the milk around to your doors at four o'clock on winter mornings. That is the coldest time in the night — those early morning hours.

24

These milk carriers never have their names in the paper on the front page. They may think of themselves as on the fourth team, but I want to tell you they are heroes. We could not get along without them. We must have milk.

A young man, who was later to be president of the United States, was graduating from college. After he received his diploma he left those who pressed about him to offer congratulations and went to the edge of the crowd, where stood a small, bent woman with gray hair and kindly eyes. He placed the diploma in her hands and throwing his arms about her said: " Here, mother, it is yours. You did it." President Garfield had had all the honors bestowed upon him, but he did not forget that it was his mother who had made it possible. She had earned money by cooking and washing, and by stinting and saving managed to get enough together to send her boy through college. She may have thought she was on the "scrub team" but she was a heroine.

This old world needs heroes like that. It needs boys and girls who will not quit because they cannot play on the first team, lead the band, or be president of the club. It needs boys and girls who will do their part whatever or wherever it may be, getting their reward in knowing that they are doing well what they have been asked to do. We cannot all be front-page heroes but we can all do our small piece of work with courage and heroism. To such heroism as this I call you.

THREE DONKEYS

And as they went their way, Jesus began to say unto the multitudes concerning John, What went ye out into the wilderness to behold? A reed shaken with the wind? MATTHEW 11:7

DID YOU EXPECT to see John swaying one way and then another as a reed is blown this way and that way by the wind? Or did you come out to see a prophet, a man with convictions? With backbone?

Have you ever heard the story of the man, his son and a donkey? I call it the " Three Donkeys."

First, the man and his son walked and led the donkey. Some people passed them. As they passed they said to each other: " Isn't that strange? Two people walking and no one riding the donkey. Why doesn't one ride? "

Overhearing this remark, the man placed his boy on the donkey's back. More people passed. These said: " Awful! A strong young lad riding and his father walking. Why doesn't the boy lead the donkey and let his poor father ride? "

Thinking it over, the father decided they were right. So he took the boy down and climbed up on the donkey's back and the boy led the animal. Presently more people passed. " Isn't that a disgrace? " they said. " Think of that man riding while his poor boy is walking. He should be ashamed of himself. Why don't they both ride? "

That is a good idea, the man thought, and he took the boy up and placed him also on the donkey's back.

As others passed, he heard them whispering: " Isn't that cruel? Two people riding on one poor donkey! Someone should stop it."

The father, hearing this, began to feel very sorry for the donkey. There was only one thing they had not done. They tied the legs of the donkey together and placing a pole through the straps they carried the donkey. They crossed a bridge which swayed a bit; the pole slipped from their shoulders and the donkey, falling into the river, drowned before their eyes.

" There," said the man, " try to please everybody and please nobody."

Some boys and girls are reeds shaken by the wind. They do not seem to have any opinions of their own, but are always waiting for someone to make up their minds for them. If their playmates do something, they do the same thing. If others go to church school, they want to go. If some of their friends stay away, they stay away too. They will join the church if someone else will join. If the others do not join, they decide they will wait until later.

Did I ever tell you of the girl who did not buy a pair of shoes — which she must not have needed very much — because she could not decide what kind she wanted? One friend pulled her one way; another friend pulled her in the opposite direction.

The truly great men and women have not been wishy-washy like that; they have had convictions. They knew what they wanted. They made up their minds and kept them made up until they found something better.

Great men do not go strutting around saying: " This must be done. This is my idea, and I must have my way." Not at all! No one likes that kind of a person. Theodore Roosevelt and Lincoln, it is said, listened to everybody and listened to no one. Which means that they asked advice of others and after getting their ideas decided upon some plan of action and stuck to it. We may well follow them. Be sure you are right and then go ahead. Be a prophet, not a reed shaken by the winds.

THE CIRCUS BAND PLAYER

*Then Samuel said, Speak; for thy servant hear-
eth.*   I SAMUEL 3:10

SAMUEL WAS A small boy when he heard this voice in the
dark. He thought his father had called him. Twice he
ran to his father and each time said to him, " Here am
I; for thou calledst me." Finally he discovered that God
had been speaking through his conscience telling him
that he was expected to do great things in his life.

Do you think it was an accident that Samuel heard
this voice? I do not believe it was. Rather, it was because Samuel was the kind of boy that could hear. To
understand the sort of boy he was, we must remember
that his mother had long before that night dedicated
Samuel's life to the service of God. Samuel knew that;
he thought about it; he went often to the temple and
helped his father in the worship services. If his mind
had been filled with useless or evil thoughts, he would
never have heard.

I suppose a cornet is just a cornet to you. Two cor-
nets look so much alike that, no doubt, you conclude
they are exactly alike. There is, however, a vast difference between them. The tone that comes from a cornet
depends very much upon the way it has been played. If
the player has been blowing hard, rough tones into it,
it is very difficult for even a very fine player to produce
mellow, beautiful tones from it. If, on the other hand,
a real cornetist has been playing the instrument over a
period of years, it is difficult for one to play a harsh note.
No one knows exactly why this is. It is said that the

quality of the tone is due to a coating which forms in the tubes after the cornet has been used for some time. But no matter why it is, we do know that a musician clings to his old instrument and protests most vigorously if anyone else tries to play it.

Some years ago I found myself playing in a band next to a man whose execution was faultless but whose tones were harsh and shrill. In conversation I discovered that he had played for years in a circus band. His cornet must have been fairly coated with wild, shrieking, circusy tones, for that was the kind that came out.

All of which is to say that we get out of anything what we have been putting into it. I heard a boy slam the door a few days ago and shout angrily, " I won't do it." I inquired into his home life, to discover that this shrill note was not an accident. He was a circus band boy. He had played into his life-cornet such notes so long that they had become natural.

The worst of it is that the change may be going on within and no one can see it. " Have you seen Alice Johnson? " a friend said to me, " She seems like a nice girl." Yes, she looks it. She has bright hair ribbons, a white dress and shining silver buckles, but she is changing. Be careful; do not cross her; give her what she wants or you will have some ugly tones. " She is all right," said another girl, " but she's awfully hard to live with." That is about the worst thing you can say about anyone. We are not all right if we are hard to live with. There is something wrong that needs to be changed.

If you want your life to give forth clear, pure notes, you will " watch and pray," lest daily you breathe unkind and impure tones into it. For a good life is not an accident; it is the result of years of careful, kindly playing.

30

A HAPPY BUS CONDUCTOR

But be of good cheer.

JOHN 16:33

JESUS WAS the most cheerful person that ever lived. Read Matthew or Luke and see for yourselves how he loved birds, trees, water, lakes, flowers, sunsets. He talked about them. He liked people, especially boys and girls. They liked him. People sometimes said unkind things about him because he was happy and enjoyed life. They called him a "wine-bibber" and a "glutton" (they meant a person who drinks or eats more than he needs, as folks do sometimes on Thanksgiving) because Jesus went to dinner parties and wedding feasts. Since he was a religious man and talked about God they wanted him to have a long, sour face.

I must tell you what I saw in New York. I was late and the place where I wanted to go was fully a half-hour's ride away. I know I looked grumpy when anyone stepped in my way. Hailing a bus, I jumped to the step. A voice said, "One seat downstairs." That was not unusual, but the way the voice said it, was. I looked up and a young man of twenty-five smiled down at me. I smiled; I could not help it.

He came in after my dime. I was reading. Several others entered, and in so doing, pushed him over against my book. He said, "I am very sorry, sir, to disturb you," and smiled. I looked up and smiling said that it was all right. It was easy to smile then; it had been hard before I started the ride.

31

Just then two women came up on the steps. I expected to hear, " Step lively, please," for they were very slow, one seeming not to care whether the bus started again or not. Instead I heard this smiling voice say, " Two seats in the orchestra, ladies." They smiled, actually hurried a little, and laughingly told two other passengers what the conductor had said. Their remarks made several more laugh.

A man next to me said, " He's a jolly fellow, isn't he? " I noticed when he left the bus at the next stop he paused to chat a moment with the young man. As he left, another man stepped on, and our smiling voice said, " Nice day, isn't it? " The man was so surprised that he stood for several blocks to talk to the conductor about the weather. Almost everyone as they left the car called out, " Good-by." I watched them for half an hour.

How many people did he make happy in that one day, do you suppose? Think, what a bus conductor can do. He did not know he was doing it, did not realize he was carrying out Jesus' words, " Be of good cheer." He might have said: " I'm too busy. What chance have I, a bus conductor, to make anyone happy? "

Last week a boy scout wrote to our Scoutmaster: " I haven't time to do a good turn every day. You see, my father died and I have to do a lot at home. I help with breakfast, and then there is my paper route; after that, school. I help at luncheon, go to school again and end up with my paper route. That takes me until dark and then it is too late. Please excuse me; I really haven't time to do a good turn every day." He did not know he was doing good turns from morning till evening, did he?

You may say, " What chance have I to make anyone happy? " Do you see, you have as much chance as the bus conductor by the cheerful way you do everything?

32

You have as many chances as you have minutes in the day. You come downstairs in the morning. It makes a difference to your father or mother the way you come down to breakfast — whether you frown or smile. It makes a difference to the boy or girl next door whether you smile as you go to school. It makes a difference to your teachers if you are in a good humor. You may not know it, as the conductor did not, but you will be making this world a happier world and a better place to live in if you will only smile and be pleasant. And it is not so difficult to do, is it? Shall we begin today, you and I, to live out Jesus' words and always — " Be of good cheer "?

PRISMS AND RAINBOWS

And he made of one every nation of men to dwell on all the face of the earth.

THE ACTS 17:26

DOES PAUL MEAN to say here that God made all nations one? That once we were all of one color or one kind and somehow we became broken up into different colors? I think so.

How many of you have seen a rainbow? At noon? No, you can never see a rainbow at noon, because it would have to be between you and the earth. The line runs from the sun through your head to the middle of the rainbow. Now you can always figure out where the sun is when you see a rainbow.

I wonder whether you know what a rainbow really is. Well, the colors of the rainbow all come from white light. Rays of light are reflected and broken up into colors by raindrops in the sky. Raindrops act like prisms. Here is a prism. When a ray of light comes into this prism it is reflected once and bent twice. When the ray leaves the prism it is no longer a ray; it is split up into several colors — violet, indigo, blue, green, yellow, orange, red. The rainbow is made in the sky by these tiny raindrop prisms. Is that not wonderful? If Paul were here he would say, " God has made of one, every color of the rainbow to dwell in the sky, for all of these colors come from white light."

" God has made of one every nation of men to dwell on all the face of the earth."

34

Do you see that the races all belong to one white light, one family, and that they are simply God's love broken up? Broken up into a sort of rainbow, for what are the colors of the races? Brown, yellow, black, red, white.

Now if all the colors of the rainbow come from white light, it would be ridiculous for one color to say, "I am better than you. I am prettier or richer than you." Each color is equally important and needed in the rainbow. It would be equally absurd for one race to say to the other, "I am better than you are because I am yellow," or "I am smarter than you because I am white." No, God did not intend that one race should think itself better than another. All are equally important in God's family.

Again, in the colors of the rainbow (which we call the spectrum) made by raindrop prisms, each color helps the other. Each is necessary to the other. This is what I mean. If I had a cylinder here with strips of rainbow colors pasted up and down around it, and if I revolved the cylinder rapidly enough, the colors would disappear and we would see only white light. The colors aid each other, you see, in making white light again.

We live in a world with many colors of men. God intended that one race was to help the other. Each has some strong point, some special kind of help to give the others. If each in a brotherly way gives that particular kind of help which it has to give, all together we form a band of loving hearts, a white band of love which reaches around the world.

Will you remember this when you see a colored girl, a Chinese boy or an Indian man? If we keep this prism in mind you and I will strive always to be kind and brotherly, remembering that we are all part of one great white light that comes from God.

35

THE SIGN OF THE CLAN

THE NAVAJO AND other Indian tribes carry tobacco pouches with the signs of their clans upon them. Sometimes it is a bear, a wolf or a coyote, depending upon whether or not the clan is supposed to have the qualities of a bear, wolf or coyote. Neil Judd, the noted archeologist, has recently dug up a pouch that is fifteen hundred years old.

The Indians are not the only ones that are carrying about with them the signs of their clans.

You have probably seen boys and girls who are like cub-bears, always growling and grumbling at things. They belong to the " Bear Clan." Either the soup is too hot or it is too cold; it is never just right. The meat is too well done or too rare; never just right. Either the day is too rainy or it is too hot; God's choice of weather never suits them. When asked to do anything at home, they always whine: " Why can't Janet do that? I'm doing something all the time." They may not know it, but these Indians wear the bear sign written on their very faces. They might as well carry a sign around their necks with large letters, " I belong to the Gloom Clan."

There is another called, " Me Want It All Clan." This is the selfish clan. This clan wants the best for itself: the best pencil, the best place in the automobile, the best book, the best page of " funnies." They never give anything away they can use for themselves.

I watched some members of this clan playing an " auto game." They did not know I was looking on, of course.

The girl insisted on moving the automobiles out of turn. The boy put his knees on the board. The girl said that the board was hers and therefore no place for his knees. Finally, both were sent to bed. They were old enough to know better, but age does not seem to make much difference to this clan. They spoiled everything, you see, including their own fun.

I wonder whether you have seen this clan: They are called, " Me No Care What Happen To Anyone Else Clan." You can see this clan a long way off. They take up the entire sidewalk so that others are pushed off. They are the " Discourteous Clan." They begin shouting when near the house, no matter who may be sleeping or talking inside. They break into conversations. You cannot miss them. They might as well hang out the sign, " I am a member of the Discourteous Clan."

There is the unkind clan. They say sharp, unkind words. They talk about playmates behind their backs. When asked to do something for the household, they snap or yap like a coyote. We may call this the " Coyote Clan "; the coyote does not know how nor when to hold its tongue.

An interesting fact about the Navajos is that they left the mark of their clan on rocks or trees when they moved to another place. These clans, about which I have been talking, leave their marks behind also. The Unkind Clan leaves tears; the Discourteous one leaves sadness; the Bear Clan leaves frowns; and the Selfish Clan leaves unhappiness.

There are other clans but I will close with one more. We read about it in the book of Acts, fourth chapter and thirteenth verse. " Now when they beheld the fearlessness of Peter and John, they took knowledge of them that they had been with Jesus." That is to say, when these people looked at Peter and John they saw that they were wearing the sign of the " Jesus Clan."

How true it is. If we really have the spirit of Jesus, wherever we go we will carry the sign of his clan. What are these signs? Just the opposite of the clan signs I have been telling you about. These signs will be: kindness in word and act; unselfishness; good cheer; courtesy and thoughtfulness. What I desire most for you is that you will wear the signs of this clan in such large letters that other boys and girls will say: " See what beautiful signs these boys and girls carry about with them wherever they go! I want to join that clan."

WHY THE FLAG FELL TO PIECES

ONE DAY I WAS calling on the Principal of our high school when my eyes chanced to light on this old tattered flag standing in the corner. " It went to pieces doing nothing," said the Principal, and turned to the matter at hand.

The story of this flag is the story of what happens in life. We usually think that we wear things out using them. " No," says this old tattered remnant, " they go to pieces doing nothing." The dentist tells us that it is not because our teeth are used that they decay. The reason for the softening and decay of our teeth is that they are not used often enough on hard substances. Our present-day food is too soft. Our teeth go to pieces doing nothing. When the doors of the dungeon were thrown open during the French Revolution, some poor bewildered prisoners came staggering blindly out into the light. In the darkness of years their eyes had forgotten how to see. They went to pieces doing nothing.

It seems to be a rule of life. If you do not use your minds, after a time they refuse to think at all. If you are too lazy to walk and exercise, very soon it becomes difficult to walk. The best way to keep anything, then, is to use it every day. It seems strange but it is true that if you wish to preserve your automobile you will run it often. Even the tires go flat when allowed to stand. Young men and women leave high school and go to college. In many cases the net of extra-curriculum activities closes around them and they neglect their studies.

39

Very often they go home discouraged and beaten. Their minds fell to pieces just as this flag did.

Boys and girls in moments of great enthusiasm decide to be Christians. They sincerely desire to follow the kind of life which Jesus lived. But they allow their flag of Christian activity to stand in the corner, and after a time they are back where they started. Because they do nothing about it, their Christianity just naturally falls to pieces.

Sometimes you and I have a desire to do something for someone else. We feel sorry for an elderly woman, perhaps, who must sit all day counting off the minutes in her loneliness. But maybe we do nothing with our desire for a few days and gradually it drops to pieces.

If we would keep prayer, we must use it. If we would preserve the purity and light of our souls, we must exercise them in ways of purity and peace. If we would keep the feeling of God's presence, we must " practice his presence " and do his will.

THE HOUSE THAT HEARTS BUILT

*For every house is builded by someone; but he
that built all things is God.*   HEBREWS 3:4

FOR MORE THAN a year now we have been watching the
building of this church. You remember, we first dug a
great hole; then the foundations were laid, and on these
the walls were erected; now we have this beautiful
church. I want you to help me for a moment. What
was needed to build this church? Mention some things.
(The class answers) Stone, cement, sand, water, wood,
iron, plaster, mortar, nails, wire, glass, lead, bricks; is that
all? Money? Yes, we could not have these other things
without money, but there is something still more important.

I shall tell you a fairy story; the answer to my question
is somewhere in it.

Once upon a time, on a lovely moonlight night a stone
was out walking when he met a stick of wood.

" Good evening, Mr. Wood," said Mr. Stone.

" How do you do, Mr. Stone," said Mr. Wood. Being
old friends, they walked along together.

" I have just had an idea," said Mr. Stone. " How
would you like to spring a little surprise on the people
who live in this vicinity? Let's get together and build a
church for them."

" Oh, ho! " laughed Mr. Wood. " What do you
mean? "'

" I mean just what I say. Let's hurry about to see if
Mr. Pain O. Glass, Mrs. Wilby Plaster, Miss Grainsy

Sand, Mr. Strong Cement, Miss Slender Wire, will help us out."

"All right," said Mr. Wood, and away they went in opposite directions as fast as they could go.

And how you would have laughed to see the sticks, stones, and glass working away all through the night! One stone would lie down, some mortar would run over him and another stone would lie down on the mortar. When morning came, here was this wonderful church. No one to this day knows what really happened in the night and how this church happened to be built.

Is that a true story? No? What is wrong? Is that the way churches are built?

You are right; there is more in this building than bricks, stones and trees. There are minds, hearts and souls in it. Paul said, "For every house is builded by someone." To build this, the thought, time and energy of many people were required. Perseverance, courage, faith, sacrifice, loyalty are in this building. Therefore, this church is not material; the materials were least important. This church is spiritual.

So, when you come here Sunday after Sunday, remember what your fathers and mothers, and other fathers and mothers, did for you and for the other boys and girls of this community. Then show your thankfulness for this gift by using it. "For every house is builded by someone, and he that built all things is God."

NUT GRASS OR COTTON PLANT?

For God so loved the world that he gave . . .
JOHN 3:16

IN A GREAT COTTON field in the Salt River Valley of
Arizona there grew many cotton plants which promised
to give a splendid yield of cotton. But there was one
little plant that was having a very hard time. It grew
near the roadway where the weeds had spread, and the
weeds had taken so much nourishment from the soil that
the little plant had to feel very far to get enough to eat.
One weed, a nut grass weed, had dared to spread its
roots into the very field itself. The little cotton plant
did not like this.

" Can't you spread your roots toward the road? " she
asked the nut grass. " There you have the whole length
of the wayside to grow."

The nut grass waved saucily in the wind. " I'll grow
where I please," she answered. " I prefer to grow where
I am not wanted and to push out weak, delicate plants
like you just to show how strong and healthy I am.
I'd be ashamed to be a cotton plant — such a delicate
thing! "

" I may be what you call me — a delicate thing," returned the cotton plant, " but with sun and water to help
me, I grow stronger as I grow older and then I am able to
serve the world because I have so much to give! "

" Bah! " the nut grass whistled. " So much to give
— what's the use of giving? It's much more fun taking.
I take everything I can get. That's why I reach so far

with my roots and twine them around your roots. What is this thing you do that you boast about?"

"I do not boast," the cotton plant said meekly. "I tell you what is true. I am glad to serve. The fine, soft cotton that the sun will help to bleach white, when these brown bolls that I carry burst, makes material for people's clothing, sewing thread, stockings and many other things that I no doubt have never heard of. And the seeds I give can be used not only for replanting, but when cleaned and crushed give an oil that is used for many things, chief among them greasing great machinery that men use in so many ways, even oiling and keeping fit the engines on great ocean liners. And my cotton seed is ground into meal and mixed with cows' food and chicken feed to make rich milk and better eggs. It is true that I am not a very strong plant, but I have great work to do."

Again the nut grass whistled scornfully.

"Well, say what you will, I am greater than you because I have the power to destroy. In no time I can take away all your food and cramp your roots so you will wither and die. It's funny how I came here. No one ever heard of me until some orange trees were shipped in here from Florida. I was hidden in some sod that was packed around the roots of one of the trees. I grew quickly here in this warm climate — just where I was shaken from the sod. For two years my roots have been spreading out, and from the little nut seeds on them other plants have grown and spread their roots and fresh nut seeds. I work underground you see. I can cut right through this field, for new plants will spread out before me."

Again the nut grass whistled scornfully. The poor little cotton plant quivered.

44

Then came a soft tread on the sod. Farmer Brown was coming; a sharp and shining scythe was in his hand. Straight to the nut grass he came, and with a long sweep of his arm slashed the grass off just above the ground. But he was not satisfied with that. He took a trowel and with great care dug out the roots and the little nutlings that were attached to it.

" You will spoil my cotton, will you! " said the farmer. " Well, we've not an inch to spare for a plant like you! "

Carefully Farmer Brown covered the ugly hole; then crushing the nut grass and the roots in his hand, he strode off to a small fire that he had built in the road and burned them.

No more the scornful whistle of the nut grass! The little cotton plant sighed contentedly. Proudly she shook the little bolls that held the priceless cotton and sent her roots creeping out into the nice fresh earth about them.

When this conversation was told me by a kind friend who overheard it, I thought, what a wonderful story for my boys and girls!

Here is a boy who comes to a lot to play ball. Some smaller boys are playing. He is larger than the others, and he decides to pitch. The smaller boy who is pitching gives up very reluctantly, tears in his eyes, for he has waited a long time for that chance. The game goes on. Finally the big boy insists that he is not out even though he has had three strikes; a quarrel follows, and the game is broken up. Which is he — nut grass or cotton plant?

A little girl who heard the story of how Jesus went about every day doing good, said, " I am very small, but surely there must be something I can do." She thought and thought, and one day she heard of a little girl living in another part of town, who did not have very much to make her happy. She saved a few pennies a week, running errands, and one day she had enough to buy something very pretty — a hair ribbon. She bought it and taking it to the poor girl, said, " Here's a ribbon that I am not going to use; wouldn't you like it? " The little girl was delighted for she had never had one as pretty as that. What is the girl who bought the hair ribbon — nut grass or cotton plant?

There were some boys on a certain street who went around together, and one day they found a little colored boy on the street. They surrounded him and began to twit him and say mean things about him. The little boy at first was angry, then he began to be afraid, and finally began to cry. Just then a boy, smaller than the other boys, rushed in and said: " If you boys want to tease someone, try me. You ought to be ashamed of yourselves." The boys fell back and he took the little fellow down the street. He was weaker than the other boys but he was very brave.

Once there was a girl who had two sisters. She really did care about these sisters, but she wanted everything for herself. They would give up to her every time. She would take the prettiest dress. She would make a scene till the best book or the most interesting page of pictures was given to her. When she came around, everyone had to give her plenty of room. She said, " Everybody must look out for themselves; what's the use of giving; it's much more fun taking." To which plant family does she belong? It is not difficult to decide, is it?

Nut grass takes; cotton plants give. Nut grass is selfish; cotton plants are unselfish. Which are you, nut grass or cotton plant?

"YEA, YEA! NAY, NAY!"

But I say unto you, Swear not at all. But let your speech be, yea, yea; nay, nay; and whatsoever is more than these is of the evil one.

MATTHEW 5:34, 37

(Use a string, winding it once about the body of a boy with arms at his side, letting him break it by pushing out his arms. Then wind the string around twice and let him again break it. Continue winding a number of times until it is impossible for him, using all his strength, to break the string.)

Do YOU KNOW what this cord represents? It is very like something which is happening to you all the time: habit. Sometimes you and I do not intend to keep on doing certain things, but we do them once, twice or three times and the habit is formed.

Jesus says: " Let your speech be yea, yea, nay, nay." Anything more than that is a bad habit. What did he mean? A person could not go about saying, " Yes, yes, no, no," all the time. We would think such a one just a bit queer, would we not? What, do you think, did Jesus mean? Well, I think he meant that boys and girls sometimes fall into bad habits of using words in their speech which are unnecessary and which had better be left out. Especially when they are angry, disappointed or surprised do they use these words. They damn the ones they are angry with, and call upon God to help them do it. Of course, at such times they hardly know what they are saying. It is mostly habit. They said these words once, twice or three times, perhaps just for fun, and then the habit became a strong cord which was hard to break.

When I hear boys or girls swear, using the name of God, it always comes to my mind that they have not enough words to say what they want to say. We call the words we use our vocabulary. Their vocabulary is not large enough. So they keep saying the same words over and over like parrots.

I knew a girl once to whom everything was shocking. The weather was " shocking." A nice day was " shocking." A view of a mountain was " shocking." If she tripped and fell, it was " shocking." It would have been better had her speech been yes, yes, no, no. There would have been as much sense to it. Every time she used the word it showed how ignorant she was.

I think that is the case of boys and girls who use the word " damn " and other coarse, ugly words. They are what you would call " dumb." They have not the words to express their feelings so they resort to these words and use them as substitutes for thought. " It is a bad habit," says Jesus. Instead of making your speech stronger, it actually weakens it.

Then, of course, no one wants to go through life shouting words like these on all occasions. Here is where habit comes in again. For what happens when we swear for a time or use coarse slang is this: the words become a part of us and pretty soon we cannot stop saying them. They slip out of our mouths when we would give the world, if we had it, to have kept our mouths closed.

Jesus gave another reason for not swearing. He said that the name of God is sacred and therefore should be used in a serious and sacred way. When we use the name of God carelessly in our speech, we are likely to get the habit of using carelessly all sacred things, and pretty soon these things are no longer sacred to us. We have lost something fine out of our lives.

Yes, you and I can get into the habit of using beautiful, strong words, or we can fill our minds and tongues with ugly, coarse, weak words. It all depends upon what we want to do. Every day we are forming habits of speech which will stay with us for years. Is it not better to follow the words of Jesus and resolve to " Swear not at all " ?

BOBBY JONES — A SQUARE SHOOTER

At Columbus, Ohio, a few years ago the National Open Golf Tournament was being played. I followed Bobby Jones around the course for two days, and saw him win from Joe Turnesa by one stroke.

Do you know how golf is played? There are those who laugh at it. " Hit the pill as far as you can and walk after it. If you find it the same day you hit it again," these sarcastic ones say. But it is not as foolish as it looks. You put the ball on a tee, a little mound of sand, and hit it with a club. You follow and keep hitting it until the ball drops into the little hole on the green where the flag is. The player who makes it in fewest strokes wins. Excepting on the tee, if the ball makes more than a half turn after you address it, that is, get all ready to play, *it counts as one stroke.*

Now Bobby Jones won by only one shot. The tournament was very close throughout. No one knew till the last whether he or Joe Turnesa would win. The second day something very interesting happened. Standing on a green, Bobby Jones addressed the ball and it moved, slightly, not enough for any spectator nor even the judge to see. But it moved and Bobby saw it. After the putt, when the official scorer held up four fingers, Jones held up five. The scorer would have given him four for the hole; Bobby insisted on the score being what it really was, five. Remember, he won by only one stroke. Win or lose, Bobby Jones set out to play the game fairly and squarely, and he did it. Best of all, Jones is modest. When asked about this incident he said, " There's only one way to play the game." He did not say what that was but everyone knew.

There is only one way to play any game. No one wants to play with a person who cheats. No golfer wants to play a twosome or a foursome with a man who keeps back part of the score. It is sometimes easy not to count a stroke when the players are separated. In the West this summer, I was told of a man who finally had to leave a golf club because no one would play with him. He would not play fairly. He would not count his strokes when he thought he was out of sight of his opponents; he found himself playing alone.

It is more important to play fairly than to win. Bobby said that to us by his action that day, and this is his lesson for us today: " Boys and girls, there's only one way to play the game of life. Play it fairly and squarely, and you will win no matter what the score may be."

WEATHER PROPHET

A cheerful heart is a good medicine.

PROVERBS 17:22

IF YOU CAN always keep cheerful you will never need much medicine; your cheerfulness will keep you healthy and well. Do you believe that? I do. This writer did.

In visiting one afternoon, a short time ago, I came upon something I think might interest you. It is a little house. Two people live in it. They are not very companionable, however, for just as soon as one comes out the other goes in. They never go out at the same time. This is the way it works. When the weather is getting ready for a storm, out comes the little man dressed in dark clothes. He represents the rain, clouds and storm. But when the weather clears and the sun shines, out comes the lady of the house, all dressed up in " Sunday-go-to-meetin' " clothes.

As I looked at it, I thought about people I knew, and not strange to say, I thought about this class. For there are some fair-weather boys and girls in this city. When you see them come out of their houses you just know the sun will shine, for they carry sunshine around with them all the time. It shines from their eyes. You can see it in their faces. Wherever they go they drive away clouds. They do not whine and crab when they go home. They open the door and greet their mothers with a happy smile and try to be of real help around the house.

But did you ever see a storm cloud coming down the street? I have. They are bad-weather boys and girls.

52

They carry a hurricane about all the time. They scowl and fight, quarrel and bicker. When they go home lightning strikes the house; it is all upset over nothing much — perhaps only a lost cap or a misplaced ball. They want everything they want, and quickly. If there is delay, there is another crash of thunder. When they go into a game with other boys and girls there are always rumblings of trouble. They form clouds for others, you see, as well as for themselves. If they could keep their clouds to themselves we should not feel so badly, but they spread their storm clouds across the sky and help make it hard for others to see the sun. Yes, sir! You can tell what kind of weather we are going to have when you see them come out of their houses.

But I want to tell you about a different sort of weather prophet. There are not so many of this kind in the city. They are precious because they are so seldom found. What are they? Well, they are exactly the opposite of the man and woman in this little house. In this way: when the clouds gather, out comes the woman all dressed up in her brightest smile with her " Sunday-go-to-meet-in' " clothes. When he sees her come out, the dark, grumbling one leaves the house and bathes in the sunshine, actually becoming happy.

And let me tell you: the one from whose home I borrowed this little house today is just like that. He keeps this weather prophet where he can see it but he pays no attention to what it says. He is always cheerful and happy no matter what the weather prophet may be predicting. He does not wait till the sun shines in order to be cheerful. He comes out, when the weather is bad, with sunshine in his heart. And the weather has been pretty bad for him. He has had storms of trouble. He is young, but for quite a number of years has been badly crippled with rheumatism. So he sits day after day, year after year, in one place. When we go to see him it makes us feel ashamed that we ever allowed a scowl to come into our faces over small matters, as we sometimes do. You see, he has chased the storm clouds clear out of the sky. He is the kind of weather prophet God wants in his world; he smiles when it is hard to smile and is happy when others would be grouching.

A cheerful heart is a good medicine. Wouldn't you like to try being that kind of weather prophet?

HOW A DOG RISKED HIS LIFE

*Greater love hath no man than this, that he lay
down his life for his friend.*   JOHN 15:13

IN THE *American Magazine* I came upon a true story I
think will interest you.

"I was reared on a farm and loved all domestic animals. One day, when I was a small child, I crawled
through the fence into the pasture. A big, four-year-old
bull charged me on the run. My yells of terror brought
'Old Shep,' who fastened his teeth in the bull's nose just
in time to save my life.

"There were three cats, fifteen cows, several horses, a
flock of sheep, two women and a man within hearing of
my screams. The animals, whether understanding my
predicament or not, paid no attention to my cry. The
women screamed and prayed and the man looked fran-
tically about him for a club or a pitchfork. But Shep,
who was more than fourteen years old, dim of eyesight
and stiff from rheumatism and old age, jumped up from
his comfortable snooze on the porch and came tearing
to my rescue with the only weapons with which nature
had endowed him.

"The bull pawed, bellowed, and shook his massive
head, whirling the old dog bodily in the air; but Shep
was offering his life for mine, and refused to let go until
I was safe outside the pasture."

Three cats! Fifteen cows! Several horses! A flock of
sheep! Two women! One man! Nobody came but the
dog.

Perhaps there were good reasons why the others did not come. We can always find reasons for not doing things if we look for them, but the fact remains that the old dog did come and save the child's life. The dog was ready, willing, eager to help, and when the chance came he did not wait for someone else; he rushed in and saved the boy. I wonder whether any of you are eager to help someone else when you get a chance.

One summer, I have been told, a man was rowing two women across a lake after dark. It was misty. There were waves but not high waves. About a mile out on the lake they discovered water coming into the boat. At first they took a hat and tried to bail it out, but the water steadily rose. It soon became serious and the man began calling for help. The women could not swim.

No one came. Just before they had heard people go by who must have heard their calls, but no one answered. The water rose steadily higher and higher. The man called; kept on calling. Finally, when they despaired of being heard, a canoe, coming suddenly out of the mist, pulled up alongside. In it were Boy Scouts, who, of all those within hearing distance, had troubled to come. They took the women and man out of the boat and towed the boat in. The Scout's motto is, "Be prepared." What a splendid one it is! They came immediately when they heard the man call; Old Shep went at once when he heard the cries of the child.

Suppose someone needs help. The call goes out. You hear it and say: "Wait a minute; I'll come. Aw! Gee! Can't you let a feller alone?" It is sometimes too late to go. Supposing Old Shep had waited! Supposing your mother is ill and needs your help. You say: "I'll help some other time. Not just now. Don't you see I'm busy?" The chance to help is lost.

There were three cats; fifteen cows; several horses; a flock of sheep; two women; one man; only the dog came. There were a number of people within hearing; only the Scouts came. " Greater love hath no man than this, that he lay down his life for his friend."

WHAT A FOOTBALL THINKS ABOUT

*But Peter said, Ananias, why hath Satan filled
thy heart to lie to the Holy Spirit, and to keep
back part of the price of the land? . . . Thou
hast not lied unto men, but unto God. . . . And
Ananias hearing these words fell down and gave
up the ghost.* THE ACTS 5:3, 4, 5

ACCORDING TO AN agreement among the people of that
day, Ananias was supposed to bring everything he had
into a common treasury and then he would be given
what he needed. But he did not do that. He decided
that he could keep part of the money for himself and
the others would never know it. So he held back part
of the price of some land. They did find it out, however. To use football terms, Ananias, when the referee
discovered his dishonesty, was penalized fifteen yards
for holding — for holding back some of the money. He
died from the shock of the penalty. His death says:
You cannot cheat without being penalized in some way
or other.

" I wonder what a football thinks about," Briggs, the
cartoonist, who died recently, used to say. It must be
pretty hard to be fallen on, piled on, kicked about,
thrown, scrapped over, for three hours. If a football
could speak our language it would tell a lot.

I was standing in front of a restaurant, a few days ago,
when I imagined I heard a voice. It was not like other
voices; this one was sort of leathery-like and a bit
wheezy, as though it were coming from a wind-bag, as
indeed it was. Looking in at the window, what should

I see but the very football used in the Mount Vernon-New Rochelle championship game. Yesterday, I went to the restaurant and the team and their Captain Lichtenberg were good enough to let me have the ball for the day.

No sooner was it taken out of the window than I thought I heard it say: "I sure am glad you took me out of that window. Anything I hate, it's that: having a lot of bozos (he is quite slangy) come up and look at me and mutter and scowl when they see the figures on me, 7–7. That means a tie, you see. Neither team liked that score, especially Mount Vernon. For the Mount Vernon team, which is a cracker-jack by the way, really made another touchdown, but it wasn't counted because the referee was wool-gathering or something at the time, and blew his whistle when he should not have done so. Wasn't there a mix-up then!

"But I want to whisper something to you," continued the ball. "That Mount Vernon team is a bunch of good sports. (So is the New Rochelle team, for that matter.) The Mount Vernon boys did not refuse to play, nor did they pick a fight with the referee or anything. They took their medicine pretty well, though they knew they were not to blame for the referee's blunder, and even though they knew that the decision was quite unfair to them.

"And the crowd! Well, after Des Marets set me down back of the goal line I had a chance to watch the spectators while the officials were arguing, that half hour, and I want to tell you, there were fifteen thousand good sports in the grandstands. Not a person booed! Not a one hissed! Not a fight! No riot afterward as might have taken place in some towns when the score was so close and both sides wanted so much to win.

59

"Do you know," said the football, "I think that was the best part of the game — the way the players and the crowd acted. 'After all,' I thought to myself, 'what is the most important thing in a football game? The ball? No, though sometimes we balls have a tendency to think so. The score? The size of the crowd? A lot of long forward passes? No, I don't think so. I think the most important part of a game is the manner in which the players and the onlookers conduct themselves. If the players slug each other and rough it up, injuring other players intentionally, if they try to cheat and get away with dishonest play, if the crowd boos and hisses and is generally unfair, in other words if they are unsportsmanlike, the game is a total loss no matter how many beautiful forward passes may be thrown or goals kicked. If, on the other hand, the teams are fair and honest, and the crowd cheers the other team and the other school and does all it can to express its good will, it is a fine game no matter who wins and what the score may be.'"

I clapped my hands to express my approval.

"I am glad to see you agree," said the football, smiling. "Speaking of playing fair and not intentionally slugging another player," continued the ball, "a football wrote me the other day that the captain of the Ohio-Wesleyan team hits the line hard, then smiles and helps up the opposing player after he has fallen. And I've been told since that there are quite a number of players in college who do that. That is splendid, don't you think?"

I did not say anything for a moment, so he repeated the question, "Aren't you going to answer me? Don't you think so?"

"Sure," I said quickly, "I think so, but let me ask you

a question. Do you think that it is right to penalize a team because one member of it is disobeying the rules?"

"I certainly do," said the football. "That's the way it is in life, isn't it? You ought to know about that. Take a boy, for instance. Let us suppose for a moment he is a team, composed of right arm, left arm, head, mind, feet and legs. He is one boy, isn't he, even if he is a whole team? If his arm gets into trouble by hitting someone when it shouldn't, his whole body is affected, isn't it? And if his mind gets a wrong idea, it makes his feet go in the wrong direction, doesn't it? Well, you see it is too bad, but the whole team, called a boy, has to take the penalty inflicted because of the dishonesty of any one of its players. Is that not true?"

I nodded again.

"And I should like to say another word about penalties," he went on. "You know how it is, when a player does not obey the rules, the ball is set back five, ten or fifteen yards towards his own team's goal. It is pretty tough on a team sometimes. Often I feel badly, but I can't do anything about it. They just tuck me under their arms and carry me back. But that is life too, isn't it? When you do not obey the rules, are you not penalized? Sometimes girls who disobey the rules of health are penalized fifteen yards — which takes them back upstairs to their rooms for several days. But it is fair, for when rules are not obeyed the one who breaks them must be set back.

"Say," said the ball, drawing closer as his voice was getting low, "I've seen some things, too, that others do not see. Sometimes when I am under a heap of players someone pushes me after the whistle is blown. That is against the rules, you see. Sometimes the man who carries me slugs someone else when no official is looking.

But I'll tell you this — I think the player or players who do this always get the worst of it. If they are not penalized in the game, they are left with a bad conscience to carry about which is the worst penalty of all."

The football yawned at this, and in doing so let out a lot of air, so much in fact that there was not enough left to talk with. Seeing this, it sort of flattened out on the table, and curling up a bit went to sleep. And I believe, like Rip Van Winkle, it is sleeping still.

WE VERSUS I

But the Lord stood by me, and strengthened me.

II TIMOTHY 4:17

DO YOU RECALL following Lindbergh in his airplane trips to Mexico, Honduras, Nicaragua, Costa Rica, Labrador, Russia and Japan? Everywhere he goes millions of people want to see him. We were proud to have him over there in Japan. Why were we proud? Because we think he represents us. It makes us feel that we are better than we are. He is so modest, quiet, sincere, honest, unspoiled, calm, brave, daring. He is the kind of person we want to be, and so we are glad to have him as our ambassador, flying from country to country.

But this is the main reason why, I believe, the world loves him so much and is so glad to see him. He is not an " I " man. He is not always saying, " I did this," or " I did that." A person who keeps talking that way, we call an egotist. Nobody likes an egotist. An egotist is usually selfish and hard.

Lindbergh always says, " We." " We were caught in a fog over the Atlantic Ocean," he said. " We did it." " We're here," he said when he landed in France. When he said that, people asked each other: " Who is the other one? Who is with him? "

Do you know who the other one was? His airplane, of course, for he flew alone. That is why it is so interesting that Lindbergh said, " We." He said it because he realized that he could have done nothing without an airplane, and the airplane could not have flown without him. The airplane needed a driver, and the driver or aviator needed something to drive. So you see, the airplane is really a part of Lindbergh. And Lindbergh is saying, " I can do all things through the airplane that strengtheneth me."

It seems to me that we should stop to think, if ever we catch ourselves saying, " See what *I* did," because it is very likely that a number of other people or things helped us to do what we did and without them we could have done nothing. How far, I wonder, would you and I get if we were suddenly to be placed on an island alone without food, fire, shelter or anything that we use every day. You might learn how to start a fire, eat some leaves or nuts for food and make a shelter. You might say, " I did it," but would you really be doing it? You did not place the trees, leaves, nuts, flint, stones or birds on the island. They were there before you arrived. These came from the Creator of the world. So if you were able to do anything on the island, it would be because God helped you. " I can do all things," said Paul, " through God who placed these things here for me." " We did it," said Lindbergh.

It is good for us to think about this because, as I suggested before, you and I grow selfish when we think that we do everything ourselves. We go to school, for example. We say, " I am getting an education." Did you ever stop to think how many people were helping us to get it? Buildings we use — who built them? Books — who wrote them? Pictures, dictionaries, histories, encyclopedias — who placed them there? And, most important of all, how about the teachers and the parents who send us? Come to think of it, we really do not do much ourselves. So we should say, " We are getting an education."

If you play a game, usually it is a game that you cannot play alone. It is interesting because other boys and girls help you play. You could not have much fun playing by yourself. If you go skating it is fun because you have skates. No one can skate without skates. To attempt such a feat would be like trying to fly without an airplane. Of course your skates could not skate without you or someone else, but you certainly do need them. So you must say, " We went skating," meaning, " My skates and I went skating."

Did you ever see a boy or girl who wanted the credit for doing something others helped to do? Well, there are such. Perhaps they were on a committee; all of the committee helped, but " I did it," says the egotist. " I made so much money last year," some man says. It is not true. A man cannot make money by himself. Perhaps he has a mill with water power. It is God's river and God's power that run the mill. If such a man is honest he must say, " We did it." Or perhaps he has a number of men working for him. These men are helping the owner to earn the money. Without them he could not have made the money at all. If he is honest the owner will say: " We, the men and I, did it. We made the money."

When we think of all this we should try to be as modest as Lindbergh. It should make us thankful to think that so many kind people are helping us to live happily, giving us clothes, heat, food from faraway lands, books, schools, churches and friends. God has given us such a beautiful world to live in. We should remember that, every day, and thank him that perhaps we may be the means of helping someone else to be happier and more comfortable. Paul was right: " We can do all things through God who strengtheneth us."

SHARK–SUCKERS

*Ye are not your own for ye are bought with a
price.*   I Corinthians 6:19, 20

Did you ever see a picture of a shark-sucker? It has
slats on it or a movable shutter-like arrangement through
which it " sucks " and so draws itself up against a shark.
When the shark swims the sucker rides along without
effort. In other words it uses the shark as a taxi, always
getting something for nothing.

The shark-sucker makes one think of some human
beings. I read of one in a McGuffey school reader quite
a while ago. His name was " Ned."

> " 'Tis royal fun," cried Lazy Ned,
> " To coast upon my fine new sled
> And beat the other boys.
> But then, you see, I cannot bear to climb
> The toilsome hill, for every time
> It more and more annoys."

The poem ends by saying that Ned watched the others
coasting by that day, and all the rest of his life others shot
past him. He was a shark-sucker; he wanted something
for nothing.

Lots of folks want castles in Spain, but they expect to
get them by dreaming. Paderewski once said, " Before
I was a master, I was a slave." He meant that it took
hours of tiresome practice before he learned to master
the art of playing the piano.

66

Boys expect to go on the diamond and suddenly become great baseball pitchers. How many realize that it cannot be done that way, that it takes hours and back-breaking days of monotonous throwing, throwing across the plate before a great pitcher is able to cut corners and attain the perfect control necessary to success.

"Everything is bought with a price," said the little Grandmother of the Russian Revolution. "You can't get something for nothing." Character does not come without effort. Good men and women are not let down out of the skies; it takes courage, practice, energy, will power and stick-to-it-iveness to be a person of character.

When we were boys in Ohio we used to fight bumble-bees to get the honey. It was a daring adventure as one or more of us usually came out of the fray with a swollen eye or a bump on our foreheads. But the sweetness of the honey was worth the price. Not so thought one of our number, however. He used to stand a safe distance away and keep calling, "Get the honey, boys." That is the refrain of all shark-suckers. By their shouts we know them.

There is something very sad about these poor fish. The encyclopedia tells us that natives tie ropes to them and when the suckers attach themselves to turtles they pull in the ropes and bring the turtles to the shore. It often happens that the boy who is never willing to pay the price for the good things of life is used as a bait by stronger men to catch other suckers.

Before we leave the shark-sucker I must tell you of another fish. It is called the pilot fish because it often swims ten feet or so ahead of the shark or other large fish, as though it were leading the way. It is supposed that it warns the shark of danger. Whatever may be its idea, it is exactly the opposite of the shark-sucker, you see, who manages always to get pulled along.

Pilot fish boys and girls do not wait for someone to drag them through life. They are alert, brave, adventurous, industrious, always leading the way to new thoughts and better action. Don't be a shark-sucker; be a pilot fish.

THE ORCHARD TEST

By their fruit ye shall know them.
MATTHEW 7:16

FATHER PLANTED an orchard. A fine orchard everyone said it would be. After a number of years the trees were all the same size with green leaves and bright blossoms. Some of the trees however never bore any fruit, not an apple. Some bore sour, sapless Ben Davises; others, juicy Baldwins. We did not know the trees until we saw their fruit. Jesus was talking about men and women when he said the words of the text. I think he was talking about boys and girls too.

Did you ever see any sham fruit? Sometimes we see imitation fruit in a dining room. It makes your mouth water, looks nice, but that is all. It is a disappointment if you are hungry. The world does not want and does not like sham fruit.

Sometimes employers write to ask me whether I know of any honest boys who want work. Suppose I should answer: " No, I don't know of any; but I have some that look as though they were honest. They have good color. They are the same size as other boys. They wear nice clothes." Would any firm hire a boy on that recommendation? Not likely. Or supposing some organization should call me and say, " Have you an unselfish girl, who could help us in some work? " And I should answer: " No, I haven't, but I have a make-believe maiden blush or an artificial peach here that looks like other fruit." Do you suppose they would take her on that recommendation?

69

Shams have a way of being found out. Sham fruit is discovered when you try to eat it. You do not test boys and girls that way, but I will tell you ways of doing it. You can tell them when they begin to play. I have many chances to watch boys and girls play. One day quite a number came to the church lots. They were smiling; they looked like bell-flowers. The game started. Soon one boy was hit and he went home crying. Soon after a girl was hurt. Then the game was broken up and all went away frowning. What was the trouble? There were several sour apples in the crowd and we did not know they were not genuine till they played. They were not gentlemen or gentle girls; they were rough russets. By their sour fruit we knew them.

About three or four o'clock on week-days, girls and boys go home from school. They look like real apples, pretty much alike. Let us select one. He laughs with his playmates, arrives home, opens the door and walks in. What a difference a door sometimes makes. Like magic he changes color. He shows what he really is: irritable, unreasonable, cross, selfish, noisy, unkind to sister and mother. He is a sham; he is not genuine clear through. We might call him a crab apple.

The way to get rid of sham is to select as an example someone who is real and true. That is why we come here. We come to look again at the life of Jesus. He was kind, thoughtful, unselfish, forgiving. When we look at him, we see the sham in ourselves and we want to be better. His life says to us: "Don't be a make-believe; don't be a crab apple; be a sweet, honest apple." For by your fruit will you be known to be a follower of Jesus.

THREE MONKEYS

*Blessed are the pure in heart: for they shall see
God.*   MATTHEW 5:8

YOU HAVE HEARD of the three monkeys carved on the
frieze of a Shinto temple at Nikko in Japan. One has
his hands over his eyes which means, " See no evil "; the
second has his hands over his ears, " Hear no evil ";
the third has his hands over his mouth, " Speak no evil."

That is all very good, but somehow I never liked the
idea of keeping one's eyes, mouth and ears shut so much
of the time. I had a better idea this week. See if you
like this better.

(Show the class a drawing of a monkey with hands
shading the eyes.)

This monkey is not closing his eyes; he is shading them
so that he can see better. He is not looking for evil,
however, he is looking for the good. His motto is, " See
the good." Nine chances out of ten, if he keeps on looking for the good he will find it in everything and everyone. There are those who are always talking about the
badness of people. Others are always seeing the good in
them. Which do you think are the happiest?

(Show the class a drawing of a monkey with hands
back of ears, listening intently.)

This monkey is not closing his ears; he is trying to hear.
He is listening for something sweet and beautiful. One
person goes to church; a discord from the organ seems
to be all he can remember in the service. Others go and
hardly hear the discord at all; they are so thrilled with

71

the beautiful harmony. " Hear the good," says this monkey, " and you will not have trouble with the bad."

(Show the class a drawing of a monkey with hands on both sides of his mouth, fairly shouting the good.)

This monkey is saying, " Speak the good." While you are speaking well of someone you cannot be speaking ill. You won't have any room for bad words if you fill your mouth with good ones. " What a nasty disposition that girl has," said one girl. " Yes, but she is good to her little brother," said her playmate. The first girl said no more; the evil words were crowded out.

That is what Jesus meant when he said, " Blessed are the pure in heart for they shall see God." Blessed are the boys and girls who are always looking for and listening to God and goodness, for they will find them. At the first and last we get what we are looking for.

MAGIC

*Passing through the valley of weeping, they make
it a place of springs.* PSALM 84:6

THAT WAS QUITE a thing to do: to go through a dry,
desert place where folks weep for lack of water and turn
it into a place of springs. These Hebrew people often
did that. When they came to a dry place they dug a
well and turned the desert into a place of refreshing cool-
ness for those who followed.

This morning, I want you to see how Beethoven, the
great musician and composer, used this magic in his
own life. He was born at Bonn, Germany, in the year
1770. His father was very poor and shiftless, a drunkard
in fact. One day he decided he could use his small boy
to advantage, so when Ludwig was only five years of age
the father invited a teacher of violin into his home.
This teacher gave the small boy lessons in the mornings
and his father took him to play in the afternoons. Sometimes the teacher and father would come home drunk
at night and drag little Ludwig out of bed and make
him play. It was indeed a valley of weeping for the
small boy, and many times during the long days of
practice Beethoven would burst into tears.

Here is where his magic came in. He turned the
valley of practice into springs of genius. Ludwig made
the most of his hours of slavish toil and soon he began
to take pride in playing music which his father could
not play. He played in public at eight years of age;
composed a cantata at ten; assisted the court organist

at twelve; became conductor of a theater orchestra at thirteen; and had his first salary as assistant organist at fourteen. So completely did he transform his early ordeal into joy that long afterward he sent funds to his poor old teacher who had been so severe with him.

Later in life Beethoven again had occasion to use the magic wand. At twenty-eight years of age he found that he could no longer hear the sweet music of life about him. He had become stone deaf. Imagine how terrible it must have been for a musician and composer not to be able to hear his own music. Many of us would have sat down and wept, and stayed there in the valley of weeping. Worst of all, in a sense he was cut off from the world of humanity and accordingly misunderstood by many folks. On occasion Beethoven was made the object of jests by boys on the street who were very rude and very ignorant of his greatness. Sometimes, because there was so much music in his heart, he would burst into song as he walked bareheaded on the street. On such occasions, he would beat time, talk to himself and even laugh aloud. Once in sorrow, he wrote: " Forgive me, then, if you see me turn away when I would gladly mix with you. . . . In solitary exile I am compelled to live. When I approach strangers a feverish fear takes possession of me, for I know that I will be misunderstood. . . . But, O God, thou lookest down upon my inward soul."

He did indeed. Beethoven was cut off from man by deafness but he was not cut off from God. The music of eternity sounded in his heart and he heard it. His finest music was composed in his deafness and loneliness.

Sometimes we say: " If I lived over there; if I were only taller or stronger; if I were clever like some others

I know, I could do great things." When you think or talk that way, remember Beethoven who made the most of what he had, and by so doing dug wells of music from which you and I are still drinking.

A NIGHT IN A BARRACKS

Perfect love casteth out fear.

I JOHN 4:18

(Objects: a gun and bayonet, haversack and canteen
from a barracks)

ONCE UPON A TIME on a cold winter night, a gun and a
bayonet in an armory had a terrible quarrel. This is
the way it began:

After the soldiers had left for the night, the gun, having an old grudge against the bayonet, said to him: " I
wish they wouldn't always stick you on the end of my
nose. You aren't important anyway; we could get along
very well without you."

The bayonet spoke up sharply. " I'm not important!
You say I'm not important? What would you have
done in that last battle if it hadn't been for me? The
soldier carrying us thrust me right through the heart
of another soldier. Guns are all right maybe at a distance, but when we're close to the enemy I'm the one
that's useful."

"You useful. Pooh! " barked the gun, just as though
he were in battle. " How do you think those dead men
we fell over on the way to the trench were killed? There
were so many men lying there our soldiers could hardly
run. It was I who did it. I made those holes in them
and tore off their fingers and arms. What kind of a war
could men have if they had only bayonets to fight with?
Bah! "

76

By this time the bayonet and gun had left their places on the wall and were dancing excitedly around each other on the floor just like two prize fighters. The gun would lunge at the little bayonet and the bayonet would leap away just in time. Then the bayonet would leap like a flash at the gun's throat but did no damage as his throat was made of steel.

In the midst of the turmoil, they heard someone cry, " Sh-h! " and both scurried back to their hooks on the wall, thinking that the watchman had overheard the noisy fight.

" Now aren't you ashamed of yourselves, arguing like this over nothing? " The gun craned his stock to see who was talking. It was the canteen.

" Neither of you is important," he said. " Why? I'll tell you why. Both of you kill. Yes, you murder. You do horrible things. You kill the fathers of little boys and girls. You make men hate one another. You tear down; you never build anything. You never help anyone to live and be happier. If you did what you were made to do you would be hurting someone all the time. You're killers, that's what you are!

" If you do not understand what I mean," continued the canteen, " let me tell you of someone who is really important. It's the haversack. The haversack does not kill; he carries food. He makes men happy by building up their bodies and taking away their awful hunger. If soldiers carried only haversacks, no one would ever be killed and just as much would be settled, for all that guns and bayonets do is to bring on new wars and make men blow one another up."

" You keep out of this," snapped the gun, " what right have you to interfere in our fight? "

" What right indeed," said a low, gentle voice. It

was so kind and so gentle that the gun, bayonet and canteen looked about them in amazed surprise. " I'd like to know," continued the quiet voice, " what would happen if no one interfered with you. You two would be scrapping all the time and tearing each other to pieces."

"Who are you?" flashed the bayonet. At this they heard a swishing sound, and who should come dragging out of the darkness but the haversack himself. The three were silent.

" I've overheard it all," said the haversack. " You were very modest, canteen, not to talk about yourself. Let me tell you something. Surely if anyone has earned the right to speak, it is the canteen. What does he do? He carries water to men dying of thirst. He cools feverish brows. He cleanses wounds; he saves lives; he makes men happy. Wherever he goes he takes with him life and not death as you two murderers do."

At these words the gun shuddered and nervously shifted his position, as no one had ever dared talk like that to him before.

" This canteen has done many kind acts," continued the haversack. " Once I saw him being held up to a soldier's lips by an enemy soldier — think of it, held by a soldier whom the dying man just a few moments before had been trying to kill. The canteen made them friends. He made them realize they were brothers. They didn't want to kill each other after that. They had love in their hearts.

"And let me tell you this: if every soldier could go to the field with only a canteen of water and offer it to the soldiers of the other side, we would have peace. For haven't you read your Bible? In the New Testament it says: ' Perfect love casteth out fear.' This is what I think that means: when love is in their hearts men are not afraid of one another. They do not want to kill, for love never kills; only hate kills."

The gun and bayonet, being a bit ashamed to hear this, as they had never read the New Testament, quickly hid themselves back of an old army overcoat. And in the nick of time, for just then the watchman threw his light full upon the hooks where they had been hanging a moment before.

To this day no one knows what happened that night to the gun and bayonet. The next morning they were nowhere to be found. One soldier said that they had been stolen. Another swore that they had not been brought back from the last camp. But the haversack and the canteen smiled and gurgled quietly to themselves. They knew that the two had left the armory just before dawn, headed for an iron foundry, determined to be melted and begin life all over again.

NOW–A–DAY MAC

*But whereunto shall I liken this generation? It
is like unto children sitting in the market-places,
who call unto their fellows and say, We piped
unto you, and ye did not dance; we wailed, and
ye did not mourn.*   MATTHEW 11:16–17

THIS MORNING I want to tell you about a race horse.
Race horses have a wonderful time in life, I think. They
have such good care, good food; their bodies are kept
so clean and so glossy. When they come out on the track
you can see in their eyes how much they are enjoying the
fun.

The horse I am to tell you about is named Now-A-Day
Mac. It was at the Bridgton Fair in Maine one summer
that we saw him. These races at Bridgton were not running races in which the horses have riders, but harness
races, the driver sitting on a two-wheeled, rubber-tired
sulky, very close behind the horse.

When the horses appeared on the track for the first
heat of the race, there were seven of them. Now-A-Day
Mac looked and acted very much like the others until
he came opposite the grandstand, then he proceeded to
slow down to a snail-like walk. The driver urged as
best he could, but the horse would stop dead still or walk
more slowly when urged too much. The other horses in
fine fettle and high spirits were up the track turning
round and round as they always do, starting down the
track toward the judges' stand, then turning back when

80

their drivers saw each time that Now-A-Day Mac was not anywhere near the starting place.

Finally Mac arrived and to the surprise of the horses and their drivers, suddenly swung about and dashed by himself toward the wire. The starter rang the bell for him to stop. At this the driver turned the horse about and he trotted back until he came to the grandstand. There he slowed again to a provokingly lazy walk while the horses up the stretch nervously waited for him to come back. The driver had a whip but he never once touched Now-A-Day Mac; he probably knew what would happen if he did so.

Well, to make a very long story shorter, at last after a period of waiting, the horses started. Now-A-Day Mac was far behind but the starter shouted " Go " and away the horses went. The crowd had laughed and booed so much at Now-A-Day Mac's expense that they were not expecting very much from him. Imagine their surprise when Mac in the last quarter of a mile caught up with the field and, beating five others, won a very close second. The horse was very fast, it seemed, but terribly handicapped by its own stubbornness and whims. It is too bad he could not have trotted the mile by himself, but you see races are not run that way, and he just had to race with others.

The next time the horses came out things were no better. In fact they appeared to be worse. The crowd jeered and shouted each time Now-A-Day Mac stood in front of the stand or walked stiffly by. The embarrassed driver must have been quite chagrined, but he smiled at all the witticisms of the crowd and clucking quietly to the horse urged him up the stretch. This time when the other horses started, Mac was left standing alone looking like a monument. He wouldn't budge. We might have named him then "Day-After-Tomorrow Mac." When the horses came back to try again, a stable boy, breaking a few twigs from a bush and walking along beside Now-A-Day, switched him till he actually started. He did not go very far, however, till he seemed to remember what the boy had done to him. So at the first turn he slowed precipitately down to a walk, while the others passed him and sped on around the track. When they were half way round Mac was reminded by something or other that he was in a race, and off he went once more like a flash. He gained back quite a bit of what he had lost but could not gain enough, so that when the first horse went under the wire, the red flag up the track was dropped — which meant that Now-A-Day Mac was distanced and could not start again that afternoon.

Here is a horse, lightning-fast, that won a close second in one heat and gained an eighth of a mile on the field while racing three-quarters of a mile — what is wrong? He is a spoiled child, moody and stubborn. He has never learned how to live with other horses and consequently can never enjoy racing with them. All his speed is going to waste because he cannot join in at the right time and play the game. He is a dead loss to his owner, and I'll venture to say that he is traded or sold to a new owner every year.

Have you ever seen boys and girls like that? Boys and girls who are clever, smart, capable, nice-looking, clean and honest, but rather useless because they have never learned how to live with other people? The trouble is they are self-centered, irritable, stubborn, big-headed and pig-headed. They want their own way when they want it. If the dinner is late they grumble; when a playmate does something they resent in a game, they pick up their marbles or dolls and go home.

If you are ever tempted to be that way, will you remember Now-A-Day Mac and how he almost spoiled the race for himself, for the other horses and for the spectators?

TWO MEN FELL INTO A LAKE

*But Jesus said unto him, No man, having put his
hand to the plow, and looking back, is fit for the
kingdom of God.* LUKE 9:62

"HE ISN'T FIT," says Jesus, "because the kingdom of
God wants men who will keep on plowing no matter
how hard or stony the ground may be."

Some folks, you know, are always looking back. They
do not meet difficult things with the right spirit. So
long as things go well they are cheerful and happy, but
let a stone get in front of their plowshares, and watch
them! They are done for. They unhitch their horses
and go home.

I know a father who loves to tell of taking his three
sons into a field to hoe corn. It was a hot morning and
the pea-vines were twined about each hill of corn. One
of these boys was anxious to try his hand at hoeing. He
whistled and sang on the way to the field, but he had
hardly started to hoe when he put his hoe on his shoul-
der and walked toward home. "Where are you going?" asked the father. "I've had enough of this," he
said. Needless to say, he was invited back to face his
hard row of weeds and thus learned his first lesson.

Not long ago I watched a football game. One team
made two touchdowns; after that, it was just as though
you took a pin and stuck it into a balloon. The losing
team seemed to be limp and pepless. They could not
face a situation where the opposing team was ahead.
On the other hand, I know of a team that never accepts

defeat. They will not believe they are beaten and consequently they seldom are. The Yale team actually fights harder after several touchdowns are made against it.

Several months ago I was told of what happened to two men who were spending the summer at a Maine lake. One of the men was standing on a pier or landing with the water about four feet deep on both sides. Somehow he stepped back and went kerplunk into the lake. Oh! wasn't he mad! And how he did rave and swear. They say you could have heard him a quarter of a mile. He pulled himself out of the water and walked along in front of the hotel piazza, swearing and cursing, with people sitting there, looking and laughing at him.

The other man was standing on another landing with water of about the same depth on both sides. He was telling a story to two friends, all the while smoking a long cigar. In an exciting moment of the story he stepped backward and landed in the water. His friends were doubled up with laughter. He arose to the top of the water — with a smile — and reached for his hat. Finally, he pulled himself up on the dock, picked up his cigar, lighted it and said, " As I was about to say, the man had no sooner felt his line straighten out than he gave. . . ." He went on with his story.

He took it with a smile; the other man took it with a rage. The same thing happened to both. There is the difference between people; the same difference exists between boys and girls.

Two boys have homework to do. One says: " Aw, this old work. Gee! I don't see why I must do it. The teacher is always picking on me. Nothing ever suits her." He takes it with a grumble. Another says, " I have some homework to do," goes at it, finishes it, and best of all makes a happy household.

A girl is asked to do dishes. Oo! You ought to see her face. She hates dishes, especially after dinner. She does not see why folks must use dishes anyway. Paper would do just as well. She always has to do dishes, her brother and sister never. She breaks a dish or two and breaks the peace of the home *because she does not know how to take hard things*. She turns her head after she has put her hand to the plow.

Jesus says she is not fit for the kingdom of home. The one man who fell into the lake was not fit for the kingdom of humor.

The team that goes limp after it gets behind is not fit for the kingdom of victory. The kingdom of life needs courageous, brave boys and girls who will not look back when something hard or disagreeable stands in front of them; boys and girls who will say with a smile: " I know it can be done. I will do it."

PACK RATS VERSUS TRADE RATS

Give, and it shall be given unto you.

LUKE 6:38

BOYS AND GIRLS may be divided into classes: getters and givers. The getters are trying all the time to get something for themselves. They want the best seats, the best sleds, the biggest piece of pie; they want a lot of money when they grow up. These are usually selfish and unkind because they are generally trying to get something away from someone else. Do you know any of them?

The givers are always thinking about someone else. They give themselves to make others happy. I heard not long ago of a girl who went each week to read to an elderly woman who had lost her sight. She was a giver. I know of a boy who gave up a Saturday morning to clean the sidewalks for a woman who was not able to do it.

Do you think the getters or the givers are the happiest? Jesus said, "Give and it shall be given you" — give and happiness will be given you. "It is more blessed to give than to receive." Blessed means happy. It is happier to give than to receive.

I thought perhaps you might always remember this if I told you about two rats. One is a getter; the other a giver. The pack rat is a greedy fellow. He takes everything he can find; he desires everything he sees. When possible, he takes things and hoards them like a miser. He is not very large, but his greed is so great and he works so fast getting things for himself that very early in life he has a nest much too large for his needs, into which he crowds everything just for the sake of having it. He is a selfish getter.

If you camp in the woods where he lives, you had better tuck everything out of sight or he will run off with it without any consideration for you. Once a man had a woolen sock taken; at another time, a part of a valuable book. By chance the rat's nest was discovered and the articles recovered. Nobody likes this pack rat because he is so greedy.

The trade rat on the other hand is different, as different as the two classes of boys and girls we are talking about. He never takes anything without giving in return. He may take a toothbrush or sock and leave a twig or some old paper in its place, but to him the twig or paper is handsome return. Rat-fashion he is trying to do as he would have others do to him, and he wants the world at large to know that he is not greedy, as indeed he is not. His actions speak for him, and most favorably. He is a giver and everybody likes him.

Think for a moment: are you a pack rat or a trade rat? A getter or a giver? As you think of these two classes, remember the words of Jesus: " It is happier to give than to receive."

THE COLORED FOOTBALL PLAYER

All things therefore whatsoever ye would that men should do unto you, even so do ye also unto them. MATTHEW 7:12

I HAD ANOTHER daydream this week. This time I saw a young man in college whose name was Bill. He was tall, well-built, a hard worker, very friendly — everybody liked him — and an athlete. He liked football best and went out for the team. He made the team quickly and soon came to be the best player in the line.

The big game came on, which was to the college much as the New Rochelle-Mount Vernon game is to our two cities, and the team was to travel six hundred miles to the city in which the game was to be played. The squad had been looking forward to the trip for several months.

The week before the game the coach posted the names of the players who would make the journey. When the players went to look the names over they found that Bill's name had been omitted. They were astounded. "There must be a mistake! Why, Bill is one of our best players," they said. "Let's go and see the coach about it."

They did. The coach told them that word had come that the team they were going to play on Saturday did not like the idea of playing a team with a white boy in the line-up. Bill was white, and so he could not go.

"Why do they object to Bill?" his friends asked. "He is just as good as we are."

"They haven't any good reason," said the coach. "They are colored you know, as we are. They are just ignorant, I think, and of course prejudiced against white boys. That is all there is to it. We feel that we must respect their wishes."

Bill felt it very deeply, of course. It was bitter medicine to stay at home when he had looked forward so long to the biggest game of all the season. His friends wanted him to leave the team and college, but he refused to do that and is still friendly to the college and to the colored boys, his team-mates.

In my dream I felt very sorry for this white boy who wanted so much to play and yet could not play because his skin happened to be of a different color from that of the other boys. I wondered whether God intended that boys of dark skin should have opportunities that boys with a white skin could not have, and wondered how I should feel if I were left out of things because I happened to be white. I awoke to find, as we often do, that I had twisted things about.

Instead of this young man being white, he is a Negro and the other players are white. He is attending one of our universities located where there are few, if any, colored schools. This year when the list was posted for one of the big games the colored boy was not included. He had to stay at home. Why? Not because he is not a good player; he is one of the regular line-men. No! He was left out because his skin was dark. His heart and pride were broken to see his team go off without him. Officials of the neighboring college denied the report that they had objected to the Negro's playing against them, but the fact is that the player for no good reason was kept at home.

How do you suppose he must have felt about it? Do

you think he understands why a skin differently colored should make such a difference? Do you suppose he says to himself — " Am I not God's child also? And if God made me black, do you not think that he meant me to play and have a good time too? Are white boys better than I just because they are white? "

Do you see how unfair this is? I wonder what Jesus would say about it if he were to walk through our cities and colleges today and see this going on. Certainly he would not say that we need to live in the same houses with colored people, Chinese and others, as they would probably not care to live with us. But I believe he would want us to judge them not by the color of their skin but by their character, the kind of mind and heart they have. For after all we are all children of God and since we are children of one Father we must be brothers and sisters. If we are truly brothers, let us learn to act like brothers.

PORTRAITS

*And as Paul journeyed, it came to pass that he
drew nigh unto Damascus: and suddenly there
shone round about him a light out of heaven:
and he fell upon the earth, and heard a voice
saying unto him, Saul, Saul, why persecutest
thou me? And he said, Who art thou, Lord?
And he said, I am Jesus whom thou persecutest.
. . . And the men that journeyed with him
stood speechless, hearing the voice but behold-
ing no man.* THE ACTS 9:3-5, 7

PAUL WAS ON HIS way to kill Christians when he saw a
marvelous picture. The picture was so brilliant and
dazzling that he fell to the earth. It was a portrait of
Jesus that came into his mind. Nobody else but Paul
saw it. It was this portrait of Jesus that finally made
Paul into a new man, into one of the greatest Christians
the world has ever known.

Everywhere Jesus went the people of his day were
taking pictures of him, not with a camera as we would
do today but with their minds. These portraits in after
years were coming up before them to change their lives.
They never got away from them. So today you and I
have pictures of Jesus helping people in trouble, healing
sick, opening the eyes of the blind; pictures of Jesus
praying, calling little children to him, picking grain in
the beautiful fields of God. These pictures of unselfishness, kindliness, brotherliness, reverence, self-sacrifice,
we cannot lose; we should be poor indeed if we ever lost
them.

Now let us see how pictures stay in our minds. Here is an interesting picture I want you to look at for forty slow counts. Do not wink if you can help it; do not look away. After forty counts look at this white cardboard ten feet away. Keep looking at the white cardboard. See what happens.

The face of this well-known young man * will come once, leave, and come again; that is, if you obey these simple rules.

Now since it is true that we carry pictures around with us all the time, I want to put this proposition to you: what pictures of you do you want others to carry about? This is important, because folks are taking pictures of you with their eyes whether or not you want them to. They see you when you are ugly as well as when you are sweet-tempered; when you are cross as well as when you are happy; when the corners of your mouth turn down, as well as when the corners turn up.

It might be, you know, that some people will see you only once in their lives. If so, how do you want them to see you? Would you like to leave with them a picture of a kind, considerate, courteous, honest boy, or a picture of a smart-alecky, sneaking, underhanded, hard, selfish, ill-natured person?

Perhaps some boy may say, " Well, what do I care? " You may say that, but down in your heart you do care what others think of you, for what others think makes a big difference. Their opinion may help or mar your life.

What kind of a picture of you do those in your home carry about? Ah! here is the real test. Your brothers and sisters are taking pictures of you all the time, and

* Detailed information concerning the black and white print of Lindbergh used in this talk may be secured by writing the author.

the picture they carry about is making their lives happier or unhappier.

Remember this then, as you leave the church today, and I believe you will try always to show to others the fine, brave, kindly, unselfish, cheerful, thoughtful boys and girls you really are.

"TELL US A STORY ABOUT CANNIBALS"

And the Spirit and the bride say, Come. And he that heareth, let him say, Come. And he that is athirst, let him come: he that will, let him take the water of life freely. REVELATION 22:17

YOU ASKED ME to tell you a story about cannibals. Cannibals, you know, are human beings who live on human flesh. They eat up other men and women, boys and girls.

I found a wonderful story for you. Many years ago in England there lived a boy who did not believe in religion. He refused to go to church. He had a strange idea that religion was for women and children. So he laughed at ministers and tried to break up religious meetings with his rough gang which followed him about everywhere.

One rainy evening there was a revival service going on, when in stamped this boy and his bunch. There was a large congregation and all were very much in earnest. The boy could see that. That made him somewhat curious. When the congregation sang, they sang not half-heartedly but as though they meant it. Suddenly, something happened. The younger of the preachers arose to speak. He looked directly at the boy. The boy squirmed just a bit. The minister said: " The Spirit and the bride say, Come, and he that is athirst let him come." The boy arose and went. " I was athirst," he said afterward, " and I came."

And who do you think this boy was? James Chalmers,

the great missionary. He taught a church school class first; the year following he began preaching; later he was city missionary; then he went to college. When he came out of college he felt that he must take the glad news about Jesus to other peoples.

He selected New Guinea, an island just north of Australia. There he did many fine and wonderful things, helping the people in every way he could. He healed their diseases; taught them how to keep clean in body and mind; and told them about the love of God. These people were afraid of everything and lived constantly in fear. Because of his work, one hundred and thirty mission stations were established there.

One day he went up Fly River. That was a very dangerous voyage as there were savage cannibals up the river. Robert Louis Stevenson heard that he had gone. He said: " It is a desperate venture, but he is quite a Livingstone card. He is a rowdy, but he is a hero. You can't weary me of that fellow. He is as big as a house, and far bigger than any church. He took me fairly by storm as the most attractive, simple, brave and interesting man in the whole Pacific."

It was Easter Sunday evening. The party had landed up Fly River near a settlement of savages. The natives came out in their canoes and swarmed over the boat. Finally Chalmers induced them to leave, saying that he would visit them at daybreak. Immediately the savages sent runners to all the villages about. Next morning when Chalmers and his party landed he was told that a feast was prepared for them. As Chalmers entered the hut, he was struck on the head by someone from behind, as were another white man and some native Christians. They were all killed by the cannibals.

Chalmers wrote in his last letter, " There will be

much to do in Heaven. I guess I shall have good mission work to do, great, brave work for Christ! He will have to find it, for I can be nothing else than a missionary." Remember, it was James Chalmers saying this, who as a boy had tried to break up religious meetings, the boy who would have nothing to do with religion. Here he is willing to give all he possessed for the kingdom of Jesus.

It should make us ashamed when we think of how little we do, how little we give, when others have done so much. How we make excuses when we are asked to do just a little act that calls for us to give up some trifling pleasure!

The call is coming to this class as it came to Chalmers when he was a boy: " He that will, let him take the water of life freely." May we hear that call and give our lives, not by dying but by living always for the happiness of others.

CANNIBAL BOYS AND GIRLS

If it had not been God who was on our side,
Then they had swallowed us up alive, when
their wrath was kindled against us.

PSALM 124:2–3

A FEW SUNDAYS ago I told you about James Chalmers, the kind missionary who was eaten by the cannibals on Fly River. He was trying to help them, but they killed him. He was thinking about them; the cannibals were thinking only about themselves.

The writer of the Psalm says, "They would have swallowed us up alive when they became very angry." I wonder what he means.

Do you know about cannibals? They were people who ate other people.

Eugene Field told us about some cannibals in his poem — "The Duel."

The gingham dog and the calico cat,
Side by side on the table sat;
'Twas half past twelve, and (what do you think?)
Nor one nor t'other had slept a wink!
The old Dutch clock and the Chinese plate
Appeared to know as sure as fate
There was going to be a terrible spat!
(I wasn't there; I simply state
What was told me by the Chinese plate.)

The gingham dog went, "Bow, wow, wow!"
The calico cat replied, "Mee-ow!"

The air was littered an hour or so,
With bits of gingham and calico,
While the old Dutch clock in the chimney place
Up with its hands before its face,
For it always dreaded a family row!
 (Now mind; I'm only telling you
What the old Dutch clock declares is true.)

The Chinese plate looked very blue
And wailed, " Oh, dear!   What shall we do? "
But the gingham dog and calico cat
Wallowed this way and tumbled that
Employing every tooth and claw,
In the awfullest way you ever saw,
And oh! how the gingham and calico flew!
 (Don't fancy I exaggerate,
I got my news from the Chinese plate!)

Next morning, where the two had sat
They found no trace of dog or cat;
And some folks think unto this day
That burglars stole that pair away;
But the truth about the cat and pup
Is this: they ate each other up!
 (The old Dutch clock it told me so,
And that is how I come to know.)

Eugene Field is telling us that it is dangerous to become angry; we may want to eat somebody up.   For
there are cannibals, you know, who eat each other up in
anger.   There may be some of those in our homes: boys
and girls who eat others up.   These cannibals are always
right in what they say or do.   If anyone dares to suggest
they are not right they become angry and try to swallow

up the household. They think they know better than anyone else. They insist on their own way. They snarl, snap, bicker, quarrel, roar, growl and generally make things miserable. Did you ever know of a boy or girl who tried to run a house? I have. They are cannibals; they eat up the rights of others. They take all the joy out of life. They trample on the feelings of other members of the family.

There are cannibals in some church schools: girls who insist on being the star in the crown. They must be chairman or president or they won't play. " I don't care," this kind always says, " I've been here the longest," or, " I'm the oldest; I'm the one that should be elected." If they cannot have their way, they sulk, pout and spoil everything. What are they? I think they could be called cannibals that eat up offices, chief places and chairmanships.

A cannibal boy or a cannibal girl is like those huge, ancient animals we read about, with necks sixty feet long. They used to lie in the middle of a swamp and eat up everything around them. There are boys and girls who stay in the middle of the house and reach about in all directions, eating things up. They are " gimme " cannibals. They are always saying, " Gimme." " Gimme this; gimme that." " Gimme some money." They take the money and buy things not because they need the articles but because they have got into the habit of wanting everything.

Nobody likes a cannibal; nobody wants to be eaten up. Cannibals never think of anyone else; cannibals never give happiness to anyone else. Don't be a cannibal.

THE STORY OF A FRIEND

A friend loveth at all times.

PROVERBS 17:17

YOU ASKED ME to speak about women who do things, and so I have selected one I think you will like. Everyone who knew her liked her. She was called a friend; her life story has been entitled, "The Story of a Friend."

How many of your acquaintances have difficulty in keeping friends? It is not so difficult to make a friend; to keep one is a different matter.

Grace Dodge knew how to make a friend and to keep a friend. I hope you will always remember her. As you alight from the Pennsylvania train at Washington and walk out of the station, you see her name in large letters over a building. Miss Dodge gave herself to girls. She was wealthy but she did not sit in her house and write out checks. There are those who give money but they do not know those to whom they give. Miss Dodge went out where girls, lonely girls, were working, and showed them that she really cared about them and their troubles. Soon they came to share their sorrows and difficulties with her and she loved them more than ever. No matter what they told about themselves, it made no difference to her. Once she said, "A friend is one who knows all about us and loves us just the same." The proverb writer says in our text, "A friend is one who loveth at all times."

She became acquainted with girls who worked long hours in factories amid heat and dust. There were so many things for them to learn about life and there was no one to teach them. (This was before the time of domestic science in schools and clubs.) So she gathered them about her every week and taught them how to sew and cook, to make their own clothes and hats, and to keep well. So many came that there had to be many classes and many teachers. But the girls wanted Miss Dodge. They said of the others, "They're jolly and fine for a good time, but if it's trouble, there's only Miss Dodge." The difference lay in this: Miss Dodge gave herself. She helped the girls, but she helped them as a true friend, and they knew it.

Miss Dodge was unselfish. Did you know that that is the highest mark of a friend? Can you imagine a really downright selfish person having a friend? One does not like to be near boys or girls who always think of themselves. They are not kind; they are usually fretful and peevish.

The girls liked to be near Miss Dodge because her thoughts were never about herself; they were always about someone else. That made her very happy. The really happy persons are the ones who desire the least for themselves. They appear to give everything away, their love, time, energy and money, but they always have more than enough left to make them happy. Some boys think they would be very happy if they had all the things they could name on their fingers. But those things would not make them happy. Happiness does not come that way.

Miss Dodge never cared to have her name mentioned. When she sent large gifts or small ones, it was all the same, the card simply read, "From a friend." Someone said of her, "She is the most prominent least known woman in America."

Miss Dodge was a friend always. She never forgot anyone. When she was ill, and when her hand was badly cramped with weakness, she wrote hundreds of letters. She was never too busy to do that. Every Monday morning for twenty years the postman stopped at the door of a little house where one of her "girls" lived with a friendly note from Miss Dodge. Another one of these girls received her weekly note for thirty years.

Miss Dodge was never too tired or busy to think of strangers in New York who might be lonely. One woman was alone in the city. She had come expecting to celebrate her wedding anniversary with her husband, but he was called away. Miss Dodge sent a box of wonderful roses, carnations and violets with a warm, friendly note to the lonely woman.

She was a real Christian. A real Christian is a good friend. If we really follow Jesus you and I will learn how to be friends, as Miss Dodge was a friend, to all the lonely people of all the world.

TRAINS WON'T WAIT

LAST OCTOBER I was going to Ohio on the Pennsylvania railroad. The train made a brief stop at West Philadelphia. Very soon into the seat across the aisle from me there came a woman who was breathless with excitement. She told the woman who sat opposite her in the section what had happened. While I was reading, I overheard.

It seemed that her husband had left his store in charge of their young son for an hour while he brought her to the station. He had carried her suitcase into the car when the train stopped, and had started with it toward the Pullman. When the conductor called, "All aboard," he had tried to get off, but the door of the car was closed. His wife had come into our car while he was looking for the conductor to see what could be done.

As a matter of fact nothing could be done. The next stop was Harrisburg and that was two and a half hours ahead. It would mean two and a half hours to Harrisburg, an hour to wait for a returning train, and two and a half hours back. It would be twelve o'clock before he arrived home; it would cost seven dollars; and his son, who expected to go out that Sunday evening, would be left in the store without any word from him.

It was a distressing situation. They looked as though they could ill afford to lose the money. But this was what happened. As soon as the woman entered the car and was seated she began laughing. To her it was a good joke.

"Pappy was caught," she said. "Now he must take a ride with me. Poor man, he meant to be so kind and here he is. But it's no use crying now; we'll have a good time."

And a good time she had. So did the woman across from her. Soon she was laughing. So were the rest of us in the car. She was so funny in her remarks that we were soon convulsed with laughter. So was her husband after he came grumpily into the car and sat down.

"But, Pappy," she said, "just think, you are going to have a nice two and a half hour ride with me. We don't have this very often; we'll just have a good time. I should have been lonely without you, and here you are by good fortune right by my side." She took his hand at this and patted it affectionately.

When the conductor came through she told the story. He took the money reluctantly. He was compelled to do that, he said, though the man could write and explain to headquarters. Presently Pappy began to smile and altogether they were in good humor when he left the train at Harrisburg. When he was gone, the woman leaned back and laughed till the tears rolled down her cheeks. She was going to visit her son in Ohio, and what a good time she would have telling him about Pappy's ride!

What a way to take an affair like that! It might have been quite disagreeable. The woman might have thought only of the money they could not afford to throw away, of the boy back in the store, or of the late hour her husband would get home. Everyone in the car would have been glum and depressed. But not so! She cheered us up, and made the world that day a little happier.

I could not help think, what a lesson there was for all of us that night. Here they were! The train had pulled out. Nothing could be changed. There was only one thing to do: make the best of it. She did, and brought cheer to many people.

It would be wonderful, I think, if boys and girls just beginning life could learn that lesson. Sometimes instead of making things easier we make things harder for those around us.

For example. Some day you plan to go on a picnic. When the day comes rain falls in sheets. No one can help it but there it is. Of course you are disappointed. Anyone would be. There are two things to do: you can be grumpy and angry; or you can say, " Well, there's no use to fuss. We can't go. I'll make the best of it."

I heard of a family that went on a picnic one day. At first everything was fine. The day was sunshiny, the air was warm, the birds were singing and so were the children. They drove quite a distance, then walked a ways through fields and woods. By this time all were hungry and ready for the lunch. But behold, when the basket was opened it was discovered that the main article of the picnic, the sandwiches, were missing. There they were far from home with only the dessert and a few fixin's for a lunch. What was there to do? Get angry and give mother a piece of their mind for forgetting? Or smile? Well, be it said to their credit the most of this family smiled, ate what there was, had a good time and went home to dinner.

Remember this: there will always be in your lives

some things you cannot change. Whatever you can make better you should change, but often some things will happen which you cannot alter. When those things come, you will help a lot if you just *smile* and try to be of good cheer.

THE GAME OF GOSSIP

The tongue is a fire.

JAMES 2:6

JUST ABOVE THIS in the letter James wrote: Behold how much wood is kindled by how small a fire.

Did you ever think of your tongue as being a fire? How is a tongue like a fire? Well, in the first place, a fire is very hot. Some tongues are very warm when they spit out hot, angry words. You cannot go near such tongues without being scorched. You may have seen pictures of a person with little flames coming out of his mouth. Angry words are like tongues of flame, says James; they burn others who happen to be near. Sometimes hot, angry words burn up and destroy friendship, and even homes are scorched and ruined by the heat of an angry tongue. A tongue, then, is like a fire in that it may speak hot words and burn things up.

In the second place, a tongue is like a fire because its words grow larger and larger all the time when they pass from mouth to mouth. Have you seen a fire start with a little smoke and a tiny flame, and then grow so big that it colors the sky red? A story grows; just like a fire, when it is told over and over. Did you ever hear your father tell of the fish he caught? At first, the fish is — this long. The next time, it is —— this long. Then it becomes somewhat like a whale, this ——— long.

Some of you must know the game called " Gossip." This is the way it is played. You think of some sentence and whisper it into your neighbor's ear. He whispers it into his neighbor's ear, and so on clear around the room. The sentence each time is said only once. What comes out at the end of the circle usually is quite different from what started. You would recognize it but generally the meaning has been changed.

On Thanksgiving afternoon we played it with sixteen people in the room. Everyone was very careful to pass on just what they heard or what they thought they heard. I am going to give you now three of the trials:

(1) The basket bender broke away. It was changed to: A bucking broncho broke away.

(2) The bear puts both arms around the tree above him. Changed to: A bad barrel of buckled pickles.

(3) Sweet Rosie O'Grady ran away from home. Changed to: The great big bozo ran away.

Mind you, everyone was listening intently to get the sentence correctly so that it could be passed on correctly. But you see what happened.

What does this game prove? It proves to me that no matter how careful we may be in telling what someone tells us about someone else, we may make a mistake. It proves that it is better not to gossip at all. For example, if we hear something that is not very nice about a playmate, what shall we do? Repeat it or forget it? I think it would be better not to tell it to anyone. There is a big chance, you see, of its not being true. It may have been changed quite a bit when Betty told Sue and Sue told Patsy and Patsy told you. If you tell everything you hear you may be dealing in lies.

Again, a tongue is like a fire in that when it utters words you cannot bring the words back again. Once spoken, they are gone forever. Perhaps you have watched a piece of wood burn. When it is burned there is just as much material as before, we are told, only it is in a different form. The wood becomes smoke, embers, gas. Some of the wood goes off into the air; some lies on the ground at your feet. Try as hard as you can you will never bring the piece of wood back as it was before you started to burn it.

Now, a tongue is just like that. Once you have spoken words you cannot go and collect them again. It is as though a wind blew through a pile of leaves and sent them out across a field. You might collect some of them, but most would be lost.

A tongue is a fire. Behold how much wood is kindled by how small a fire.

FIRE

And the law of kindness is on her tongue.

PROVERBS 31:26

Do YOU REMEMBER what we talked about last Sunday? " The tongue is a fire." First, because it may become very hot and spit out angry words; second, because its words grow larger and larger as they are carried from person to person, just as a fire grows larger and paints the sky red; third, because its words cannot be gathered up again. Once spoken, they are gone forever.

After the service someone said to me, " But how about good words, kind tongues — aren't they like fire, too? " I said, "Yes, of course, but I was talking only about bad words. That was a mistake." Indeed, good words *are* like a fire; they grow just as rapidly as evil words, in fact I think they run more swiftly.

You remember when Lindbergh flew across the Atlantic? That was a brave, daring thing to do all alone. How quickly we learned the kind of young man Lindbergh was. Words about him just flew over the country. Folks everywhere were saying that he did such a marvelous thing because he had lived such a clean, wonderful life. You remember that. Ah yes, we must not forget — the tongue may be and is a fire of kindness.

And good will. Does that travel? Let us see about that. A long time ago one holy night a child was born in a manger in a Bethlehem stable. The Scripture says that the heavenly chorus sang, "Glory to God in the

111

Highest and on earth peace, good will among men."
And how those words have traveled! The shepherds
first heard them out on the hills. Quickly they told
others. Then the disciples began talking to others
about Jesus. After Easter, when they were sitting together, it was as though a wind swept through the room.
The disciples looked at each other and it seemed to
them as though tongues of fire were resting on their
heads. They called it Pentecost. Something happened.
Their tongues became fires and out they went into the
world to talk about Jesus, the kind of life he lived, the
love they had found in Jesus' life, and the peace which
the shepherds found on the hills.

Today the fire is still burning. Wilfred Grenfell took
the love of God when he went to the poor people of
Labrador who had little food and no physician. He was
a doctor for them and a true friend. And a few years
ago when General Booth was asked to cable one word to
his workers on Christmas day, what word do you think
he sent? " Others." What a wonderful word that is!
He wanted his Salvation Army workers to forget themselves and think of others. For that is what Jesus did.
That is why, when we celebrate his birthday, we bring
these white gifts which you are to bring next Sunday
afternoon. You bring what you would like very much
to keep yourself but give away to some boy or girl who
does not have as much as you have. In this way you
truly celebrate Christmas. Christmas, above everything
else, is a time to give.

And how that splendid word " others," which General Booth sent, did travel. It jumped, leaped, swam,
sizzled through the air, by wireless, cable, telephone,
to Canada, Australia, China, India, Europe, Russia,
South America, Africa. " A tongue of fire." Indeed it

is. Your tongue, too, may be a fire to make others blaze with happiness; to take loneliness from some strange boy or girl; to cheer up someone who is feeling sad; to speak words of love and kindness. Think this Christmas what a lot of good you can do in the world simply by saying nice things about your friends and playmates. Start saying to yourself the word " others "; then do something for others; and you will have a merry Christmas.

TACKLING

Quit ye like men, be strong.
I CORINTHIANS 16:13

THAT IS TO SAY, behave like real men; do not be weaklings.

Paul was not referring to a football game when he wrote this, but I want to talk about a football this morning. Have you ever wondered how a football feels? When a player kicks it hard, it must say: " Umph! what a jolt that boy gave me then. But isn't it glorious sailing through the air like this? Oh, I wish I would never come down! Why! that stupid fellow dropped me and here I go rolling around in the dirt. They're after me, twenty of them. There's one on me now. Ugh! he fell hard. It it hadn't been for me he would have been hurt. Ouch! I wish they wouldn't pile up on me that way. It almost knocks my wind out. Thank goodness, they're off now. I'm always glad to hear that whistle. It means unpile."

I wonder how many of you have seen a football game. Eleven players line up facing each other along a line, close together. One side has the ball with four chances to take the ball forward ten yards. They can carry, throw or kick it. If a player carries the ball, the opposing players try to stop him. They usually throw their arms around his waist or legs and drag him to the ground. This is called tackling, and the one who stops the man carrying the ball is called a tackler.

There are good tacklers and poor tacklers. Some

114

boys are afraid to tackle; they may be good players otherwise, but they are not placed on the teams. Other boys do not tackle hard enough; they slow the runner up a bit, but he runs on just the same. It is hard for such boys to stay on a team. Some better tacklers are likely to be put into the game in their places.

A few weeks ago we read that the Army team at West Point had some men who were not good tacklers. They sidestepped when the ball-carrier came along and let him go by. They were put back on the third team until they stopped their sidestepping.

Now I would like to have you think for a moment that we are playing a game. That game is called life. We play it from the time we awake in the morning till we fall asleep at night. It is a thrilling, exciting game: getting into our clothes without a murmur or a kick, eating breakfast, hurrying to school, doing a lot of hard study, playing after school, running errands, helping about the house, listening to the radio, teasing the cat — what fun it all is. It is just like playing football. Some boys and girls do not make fun out of it, mostly, I think, because they are not good tacklers. They do not play hard enough. They do not tackle a hard task as though they were going to accomplish it. They side-step and let the runner go by. Sometimes they are cowards, sometimes they are lazy. Whatever it is they ruin the game for themselves.

For example — down the field comes someone carrying the ball. He is running fast. Who is it? It is a hard problem in school; a bit of difficult homework. Instead of saying: " Here he comes — old man home-work; I'll hit him so hard he'll never know what struck him," the quitter sidesteps, yawns and lets the runner go by.

115

Here comes another runner with a ball. Who is it? It is a lot of weeds in the garden to be pulled. It is a hot day and there are lots of other, easier things to do. Does our sidestepper tackle the runner with a will? He does not. He steps aside and plays badminton or goes swimming and so does the easy things. He will never make the team doing that.

Here comes a very speedy runner with the ball. He is hard to stop. The girls will recognize this one. It is a room to be tidied up and beds to be made. The easiest thing to do is to step aside and put it off until later. But by that time, the game will be lost. So there is only one way out for a good player. She steps in, tackles hard, and it is over in the twinkling of an eye. The room is neat and clean and the beds are made without a wrinkle anywhere. For, if once we sidestep something that is hard to do it is harder than ever the next time to tackle it.

A boy came out of the house one day. He had been sleeping. Outside, a neighbor boy was chopping wood. "Oh, bother!" said the first, "why are you always chopping wood? Come on and play. Why do you spend so much time chopping up these old hard knots? Isn't it awfully tiresome?"

"No," said the boy chopping at the knot all the time, "when I come to a hard knot, I say, 'Mr. Knot, you won't beat me. I'm going to chop you up into kindling wood.' I just can't stop till I do it."

"Oh!" said the other yawning, "I'll tell you what I'd like. I'd like to go to sleep and wake up a rich man."

Which do you think became a rich man? The knot-chopper or the yawner? The tackler or the side-stepper? And which do you think will do most for the world? A boy who does just enough work to get by in school, or one who tackles every day's lesson as though it were a hard knot he intended to split?

This old football has a good lesson for us. It says: "Tackle hard; don't be a sidestepper. Play up, play up, and play the game!"

OUT OF FOCUS

But one thing I do, I press on toward the goal, unto the prize of the high calling of God in Christ Jesus. PHILIPPIANS 3:13–14

THERE IS MUCH to learn about a kodak before one knows how to take good pictures, but there is one thing that is most important. It is this: if I want to get a clear picture I must focus; that is, I must select some one thing out in front of me, and set the lens to take that. If I were to try to take all of you at the same time I would not get any one of you very clearly. If I focus on those farther away, those near me will be blurred.

Here are two prints. One is blurred because the one who took the picture did not focus on one thing. The other is clear: one object was selected.

This blurred film is like the lives of some boys or girls. They are not in focus. They never select some one worthwhile thing to do and do it. They come home from school and soon everything is blurred. They have homework; but there are parties, coasting, crossword puzzles and football, and well — when the day is over nothing worthy has been done.

Once there were three brothers who set out to make an engine. Growing tired of that after a time, they thought they would try to make a wagon. A bicycle came next, and finally they ended up by making a crooked stick.

Do you remember the story of the rich young man? He was good-looking, lovable, courteous, well thought

118

of in his community. " One thing thou lackest," Jesus said to him. What was it? Focus. He had a good kodak and a good lens, but his picture was blurred. He had never centered all the good things he had on the accomplishing of one worthy object. When Jesus asked him to be his disciple the young man went home with a sad heart.

One evening, some years ago, a young boy kneeled in the shadow of a church in New York and prayed. Arising from his knees, he went out to help the world. It was the great purpose of his life. He focused on one thing. Jacob Riis always had a clear picture of what he wanted to do. As a result he helped to clean up Mulberry Bend and did many other splendid things.

If you would have a clean-cut, clear picture, focus on one great object. Let that one aim be to live the kind of life that Jesus lived. If you do that, the picture of your life will not be out of focus or blurred; it will be clear and beautiful.

THE STORY OF A TRAVELING BAG

*And I also say unto thee that thou art Peter, and
upon this rock I will build my church.*

MATTHEW 16:18

THERE *was* something good about Peter. Jesus believed in him. He believed that Peter would some day
become a rock of strong, dependable character; that he
would grow to be courageous, brave and true. And
because he believed in Peter, Peter did grow to become
rock-like. Years after, he died for Jesus whom he had
several times deserted.

That is what trust did. Jesus trusted Peter, and Peter
knew it.

I wish I could help you see how necessary trust is to
you and me. We could not live without trust. We trust
someone all the time. This minute you believe that
there will be a dinner for you after this service, at home
or somewhere in Mount Vernon, do you not? You trust
your fathers and mothers to that extent. They trust you
and believe that you will go to school in the morning
and return in the evening. When you step on a train
you have faith in the motorman. If you did not trust
him you would never ride. You trust the banker when
you put your money in a bank. You believe he is honest
or you would not let him have your money to care for.
Yes, we could not live without faith in others.

I must tell you about a traveling bag. During the
last war, when the Germans came into Russia, the trains
were crowded with people trying to get away. A black

traveling bag, containing a watch, pictures and other valuable articles, was left on a train running between Petrograd and Moscow. One year afterward I had a message from San Francisco. The bag had turned up. It had been found in a Moscow freight barn, had traveled by itself six thousand miles to Vladivostok, by transport to San Francisco, then by train to Cleveland. The bag was open but not a thing was missing. How many people must have handled that bag! The journey of that bag was made by trust. Without honest folks who could be trusted, the bag would never have left Moscow.

One of the worst things you can say about a boy and girl is that you cannot trust them. They cannot be relied upon. They may not tell the truth. They may not do what they said they would do.

On Prospect Avenue there is a store where papers are sold. Because the stand is outside and folks are in a hurry those who want papers place the pennies on the stand and take a paper. Do you see, the storekeeper does this because he trusts the folks who go by? Evidently most people, most boys and girls, can be trusted.

I was told, however, that a certain boy goes up to the stand, pretends to read the headlines and slyly slips some of the pennies into his hand and then spends them at the corner store. Other boys have seen him do it. Would you trust that boy? Do you think people will trust him when he grows to be a man, unless he changes his ways? How will these boys feel who have seen him take money? And whom is he hurting? The storekeeper? Yes, a little. But mostly himself. He is making a cheat out of himself and a person that no one can trust. Let a boy do this three or four times and he has a habit that is hard to break.

Now let me tell you another story. Last week two boys came into the church office looking for me. They were quite excited, my secretary said, and they had several dollar bills in their hands. They said that they were playing ball and a missed ball had broken a window. The secretary thanked them and said that when the window was fixed they could pay for it. That is the first time any boy or girl has come to the church to pay for a broken window, and windows have been broken fifty times perhaps in the last ten years.

I have not seen these boys. I do not know who they are, but when they grow to be men, if I were an employer I should want them to work for me. I could trust them. They would not run away to dodge responsibility. They would be willing to step up and face the music. I would believe in them.

That is the kind of men and women, boys and girls, Jesus wanted. That is the kind he wishes us to become. And he is saying to us just as he said to Peter: "You, too, may become a rock of trustworthy character, and on your trustworthiness I will build my church and my kingdom." A good scout is trustworthy. A good Christian is trustworthy.

FULL STOP

And he sat down and called the twelve; and he saith unto them, If any man would be first, he shall be last of all, and servant of all. MARK 9:35

THAT IS, if any man would really be a big man, if boys and girls would be great, they must learn to be servants, to wait on others. That is not what many of us boys and girls are doing, is it? A girl in this class said once; " I don't like that Golden Rule. We kids don't do things that way. Do unto others as you would have them do unto you. Huh! No good! "

No, I do not believe many of us do things that way. You have all seen those full stop signs at our street crossings, have you not? Why are they there? To avoid accidents. To remind some automobile drivers that there are other drivers on the streets. And yet what happens? I have seen cars never once slow up but go at tremendous speed past these signs.

Last Sunday, I am told, there was a terrible accident at the corner of Prospect and Fulton avenues. Two cars were smashed up. A number of people were terribly hurt. Why? Because neither car wanted to be last; both wanted to be first. Both drivers insisted on doing just what they pleased. Both were driving too fast, and one driver paid no attention at all to the full stop sign. The sign might as well have read, " Drive forty miles an hour at this point." Do you know that we can tell what kind of folks people are by the way they drive automobiles? Some are always pushing others off the road. " Road hogs " we call them.

123

To speak of full stop signs being set up in the lives of boys and girls, is another way of saying that there are certain times when we must stop and let others have the right of way. Our brothers and sisters, our playmates, have wants and needs too. We must constantly remember that we are not the only ones to be served at the table, not the only ones in the house to be pleased with the radio; others may not want to listen always to what we like best. In a word, boys and girls must begin early to learn that a happy life comes in remembering others and in being kind and courteous to them.

Jesus says that the one who obeys these "full stop" signs really comes out better in the long run. The one who is last shall be first. A long time ago I heard a story about a girl named Gretchen. She belonged to a family that was very poor. She was quiet and kind, and very unselfish, always stepping aside to let someone else have the right of way, always giving to someone else what she would have liked for herself. In the little town where she lived many knew about these qualities in her and loved her for them.

Hard times came. Factories shut down and many people were out of work. Soon there was little bread for hundreds of folks. Those who had it, however, saw to it that others did not starve. They opened a station and stocked it each day with bread. There once a day the people were invited to come to receive their ration. Gretchen went to get bread for her family. While the other boys and girls were pushing, jostling, fighting for a first place in line, Gretchen would stand aside and wait. Then, after they were gone, she would step up and, thanking the man, go joyfully to her home.

One day a strange thing happened. The first boy in line received a small loaf. The loaves grew larger, however, as each boy or girl passed the window so that when Gretchen stepped up, a very large loaf was handed to her. She said timidly that it surely could not have been meant for her, but the kind man insisted that it was. When her mother cut the loaf open, a large gold piece fell out.

" Oh," said her mother, " Gretchen, what have you done? Hurry as fast as ever you can and take the gold piece back to the man." Gretchen fairly flew. The man was there; he was expecting just that.

" No," he said with kindly eyes, " it is not a mistake. We want you to have it. Take it to your mother and tell her to buy clothes with it."

You and I may not receive gold coins when we obey full stop signs, but we will receive the joy that comes in remembering others. He who would be first, shall be last of all and servant of all. Was this what Jesus meant? Think about it this week.

THE WRECKED HOUSE

> *Every one that cometh unto me, and heareth*
> *my words, and doeth them, I will show you to*
> *whom he is like: he is like a man building a*
> *house, who digged and went deep, and laid a*
> *foundation upon the rock: and when a flood*
> *arose, the stream brake against that house, and*
> *could not shake it.*   LUKE 6:47, 48

A FEW WEEKS AGO something occurred which made a
deep impression upon this church building. Some
pieces of rock were thrown from across the street by a
strong blast into one of the leaded windows. It would
have done serious damage to anyone passing along the
street. The blast blew a talk right into the church, so
of course I had to use it.

Have you noticed how deep they are digging and
blasting over there? Do you think it is a waste of time?
"Why don't they build the house," do you say, "instead of working way down beneath the surface?"
Why? Because you cannot make a house stand straight
and solidly unless you do have strong foundations.
When the house is built we will not see the foundation
at all, but all the time down under the surface it will
be doing its necessary work.

Did you ever think that you are building houses in
your lives? I do not mean with brick and mortar, wood
and nails, but with thoughts, words and deeds. And
just now you are building the foundations. You are
digging at school, at home, at church, getting ready, I
hope, to build a fine structure, a beautiful building.

126

Some boys and girls think they can build their houses of character on earth without digging. They do not want to study at school. Only " grinds " do that. Some boys do not care to help with housework. Only " sissies " do that. They dislike to go to church or church school. They say churchgoers are " Puritans."

Later in life when they attempt to do great things, they find that they cannot because they have not prepared themselves.

(At this point, with blocks a miniature house may be built which collapses a little later because a paper block is used.)

A short time ago a young man was discovered to have taken one hundred thousand dollars which did not belong to him. Apparently he was all right in other ways. There was a bad stone in his foundation. He was not honest, and the whole structure fell.

Not long ago I saw in a newspaper the picture of a building, one corner of which had given way. The house was almost new. The corner was wrecked because dishonest work had been done; a faulty building block had been put into the foundation, which crumpled, letting the pillar down.

I remember a young man in college. In his sophomore year he was the fastest runner in the state. In his senior year he did not win once. He ruined his breathing by smoking too many cigarettes. He had put a faulty stone in his foundation years and could not build an athlete on it. His house fell with a great crash.

Do you want to build a tall, strong building? " You must dig deep," said Jesus. It is said that skyscrapers have foundations one fourth as deep as the buildings are tall. The taller the building of character, the deeper you must go. Paul gives a wonderful suggestion: " For other foundation can no man lay than that which is laid, which is Jesus Christ." To build upon him means to put loyalty, reverence, kindness, helpfulness, giving, patience, honesty, into your foundations. Storms will never beat down a house built upon such rocks.

When your life is built and you are grown to be splendid citizens you will not see the foundation at all, but down in your hearts, you will know that you could not have built had it not been for these days of digging and working when you set into place strong foundation stones of character.

THE MIRACULOUS BOTTLE

Be not overcome of evil, but overcome evil with good. ROMANS 12:21

DO YOU KNOW how to get the air out of this bottle? Will the air fall out if I turn it upside down? Can I blow the air out? No, there is just as much air in it as before. How about trying to pump it out? Well, that can be done if you have the proper apparatus. The x-ray is made by an electric current being run through a vacuum tube, that is, a tube from which all the air has been pumped.

There is another and better way, however, to get the air out of a bottle, and that is to pour water into it. As you pour the water in the air comes out. How simple and easy that is. I wonder whether that was what Paul meant when he said, " Drive out evil with good." " If you have evil in your life bottle," he says, " pour some good in and the evil will run away."

Try it some time. When you have been very angry and wanted to chew nails or something, has your mother ever told you to stop and count twelve? Why did she say that? I think it was so that some good thought would have time to come in and drive the anger away. When you are about to frown, pick up some smiles and pour them in, and see how quickly the frowns fly away.

Paul was right. One day a boy hurts you. You feel like striking him or doing something mean to him. How will you keep yourself from doing that? By turning your mind upside down? No, that will not do it.

By pumping out the desire for revenge with your will-pump, and saying, "I will get rid of that desire to hurt him"? No, there is a better way than that. Pour a kind thought in; return good for evil, and the person who hurt you will be ashamed of his action.

Out in Ohio there is a deserted village. Weeds are growing over the doorsteps and the foundations are rotting away. You open the door of a house and step in. Mice and rats scurry about; cobwebs cover the windows. Now, supposing we wish to get rid of the vermin, what would be the best way of doing it? Take some ferrets and cats and let them catch the rats and mice? They would help no doubt, but the best way to drive out the vermin would be to have the people move back to town. Pour people into the front doors and rats and mice will go out the back.

In the spring the low-lying fields of Ohio are covered with pea-vines and weeds. The farmers plow and hoe, however, knowing that the corn which they have planted will soon spring up and crowd the weeds out. It does. In July the corn covers the entire field so that the weeds are squeezed out. Pour corn in and vines are lost. Cultivate grain and weeds will go.

Likewise, cultivate good, and bad will go. So, on a rainy day when you are peevish, do something. Read a book; write a letter; run an errand for your mother. It will work like magic.

Chase away the frown with a smile; drive away the grouch with a grin; put good in and the bad will soon die. If you do this, you will understand what Paul meant when he said, "Overcome evil with good."

WHAT MY FOUNTAIN PEN SAID

*And the foolish said unto the wise, Give us of
your oil; for our lamps are going out.*
MATTHEW 25:8

THERE WERE FIVE foolish virgins and five wise ones going to a wedding. The foolish ones carried no extra oil
for their lamps; when the oil burned out, they were left
in the dark. But the wise carried extra oil so that when
their lamps burned low, they had plenty at hand. When
the bridal procession came along, they joined it and entered in; the foolish virgins were shut out.

Every day for a number of years I have been writing
with this pen, and I did not know it could talk till Fri-
day. It was when I was wondering what I had better say
to you today, that I heard something whisper: " Hello."

" Hello," I said, " who are you? "

The voice said, " I'm your fountain pen. Listen, why
don't you use me? I've a splendid lesson in me for the
children's talk."

" Yes? " I answered. " Tell me quickly before you forget it."

It began talking in a whisper that sounded just like
someone writing on rough paper. When it finished,
sure enough it had said a lot of words on this paper, so
I'll read it to you just as the pen told it to me.

" Do you know what the difference is between the
other pens on your desk and me? " it began.

" I'm not sure what you mean. Tell me," I said.

" Well," it said, drawing itself up till I could see the
ink swelling on the inside, " I am a fountain pen. You
don't have to keep sticking me into ink bottles all the

131

time, do you? You can carry me around with you, too, and when you want to write, I am ready. I'm like those flashlights you read about in the papers — 'Ever-Ready.' I write more evenly, too, than the other pens," it continued looking at them scornfully, "because the ink flows from me constantly. With those pens, the writing grows dim after a few words. There are no fountains attached to them. They aren't ready when you need them. There is no extra supply of oil, and it soon burns out. They're just like the foolish virgins you read about in the Bible, don't you think?"

I was not thinking then, I was assenting. "True," I said, "but where is the lesson for boys and girls you mentioned?"

"Listen," it fairly screeched the word. "Some boys and girls are like those pens," pointing to those on my desk, "they never carry an extra supply of anything. In school they just study enough to pass, just enough to fool the teacher and make her think they know a lot. They have a little ink in their minds but not enough. When they really need it later in life, they run dry. They haven't any surplus. They solve one problem, but they use all their ink on that. When a harder one comes along, they aren't ready because they didn't study when they should have worked. They wasted their time and laughed about it."

"Yes, I believe that," I said, "but how are you any better?"

"Me?" it said surprisedly, "I've already told you. I have a fountain to draw on. Boys and girls who are like me have fountains of knowledge and wisdom which they have filled up in school days. When they meet some harder problem they solve it, because they have more than enough to get by."

132

" Go on, Mr. Pen," I said, " I'm interested. What else? "

" While I have been writing," it scratched, " I have been thinking that I know some other boys and girls like those inkless pens. They are not very kind. They are liable to lose their temper at any moment. They have just enough kindness to help them when someone steps on their toes, but watch out! Let brother or sister get something that they want, and they lose their heads. They grow angry, very red in the face, and stamp their feet. Why? You see it's because they haven't enough kindness and goodness stored up. Their ink of kindness soon runs out. They haven't a fountain of goodness to draw on as I have. These children may do something for someone else occasionally but they are usually selfish for their unselfishness fades out. You have to keep dipping them into ink all the time to make them write. On the other hand," the pen went on, " fountain pen boys and fountain pen girls have the ink of unselfishness in their hearts all the time, and it seldom runs out."

" It does run out some time, do you mean to say, Mr. Pen? " I asked.

" Oh, yes! The best of us run out of ink now and then," it answered, " but when we do, we can be filled up again. When a boy or girl runs out of kindness, he can fill himself or herself again, for children like me are self-fillers. In church or by prayer, they can dip themselves in the kindness and love of God and then write all week. You tell the class for me, will you, that I wish they would become fountain pens and keep writing always kindness and helpfulness."

Suddenly, the pen stopped talking and has said not a word since. But I thought it was quite enough. Don't you think so?

THE LOST DENARIUS

*Then saith he unto them, Render therefore unto
Caesar the things that are Caesar's; and unto God
the things that are God's.*   MATTHEW 22:21

THE SMART MEN of the town were trying to trip Jesus.
So they asked him a trick question. Should they or
should they not pay taxes to Caesar, " tribute " as it was
called then. If Jesus said, " No, they should not pay
tribute to Caesar," they would tell Caesar's men and
have him arrested. If Jesus said, " Yes," they knew the
common people would turn against him for all of them
hated Caesar and his Romans and the people would turn
against anyone who favored paying tribute to Rome.

But Jesus refused to fall into their trap. He said,
" Show me the tribute money." Someone gave him a
denarius. Holding it, he said, " Whose picture is this? "
The smart men answered, " Caesar's." " Give to Caesar
that which belongs to Caesar and to God that which belongs to God." A clever answer, was it not? It was
what they deserved. They left Jesus, for the folks around
were laughing at them.

Here is a real denarius, worth about as much as our
penny. This denarius was used in Palestine when Jesus
was twenty-two years of age. It is one thousand nine
hundred and seven years old. For two years this denarius was used and then the people hoarded it, or collected this and others like it and hid them. This one
was found in Sicily, an island in the Mediterranean Sea.
It was in an earthen vessel when found.

How interesting it would be to know its history, to know who handled it, who carried it about in a bag. Jesus may have held this denarius in his hand or carried it for change. Perhaps it bought food for someone who was starving. It may have been taken from the man who was robbed by the highwaymen on his way to Jericho. Maybe it was this very denarius that the good Samaritan gave to the inn-keeper when he told him to take care of the wounded man till he returned. It may have been the coin Jesus was thinking of when he said that a woman lost one and searched all through her house till she found it. It is not easy to find a denarius or penny like this on a clay floor in a dark house. Matthew may have collected this coin as he sat at the toll gate at Capernaum where Jesus called him to be a disciple. Matthew collected tribute for Caesar. Finally, perhaps someone hoarded it, as a miser does, and took it to Sicily where it was hidden away in a vase.

Now this is what I want you to see: *how helpless this denarius was all the time.* It could not help itself one bit, could it? A coin has nothing to say as to where it is to go or what it is to do. Sometimes perhaps this penny helped someone; sometimes it may have been used to buy spears or axes to kill men in war.

It all depended upon the user, did it not? Do you see that? This coin in itself is neither good nor bad, but the one who uses it may turn it into something good or bad.

For example: I have heard that a boy one Sunday morning was given ten cents to bring to church school. His mother expected him to place it in his envelope and drop it into the offering plate. He knew that his mother expected that. Instead what did he do? He spent five cents of it at a store for something he ate in a few minutes. Was that five cent piece a bad coin? No. It happened to be in the hands of a dishonest boy. Did the boy rob God by doing what he did? Perhaps; but worst of all he robbed himself. When he spent the nickel he threw away some of his character and a bit of his good name. Character, you know, is that which you really are in your heart.

It depends, you see, upon how money is used. One boy says: " I shall get all the money I can in life." He keeps this idea always in his mind. As he grows to be a man that is all he thinks about. He gets all the gold he can lay his hands on. He thinks of money day and night. If anyone asks him to give some money to help someone else, he gives a little but keeps all the rest because he does not want it to slip out of his hands. In time this is what happens. He turns into a denarius or piece of gold. He has a gold mind. He has a gold heart. Gold glitters but it is very cold and inhuman. Gold cannot sympathize or pity, be glad or shout for joy. Finally he sees nothing but money; he knows nothing but money; he cares not a fig about anything but money. He dies of money on the brain. Why? Because he did not learn as a boy how to use his money rightly.

Here is another boy. He says, " Money I want. I like money. I must have it. But money is to be used in the right way. It is not to be spent solely on myself; it is to help men and women, boys and girls, to be healthier and happier. Money is one way of bringing in the kingdom of God."

As this boy grows to be a man he remembers this always. When he spends a dollar on himself he gives three to someone else. He is known as a kind, generous man, always trying to find better ways of giving. In fact his life comes to be a gift to the world, very like that of Jesus. When the community needs money to take care

136

of its hospitals, day-nurseries, charities, he is always ready. When the church needs money he is ready and anxious to help out. Because he realizes that money is not his but belongs to God, he renders or gives unto God that which belongs to God. He is always the happiest man in the community for he knows how to use his money.

TWO WAYS OF TREATING A NEIGHBOR

But I have called you friends.

JOHN 15:15

JESUS SAID that to his disciples. " Friend " — what a wonderful word that is! I am coming to think it is one of the most beautiful words in the English language. If we were to have a vote as to which word folks like the best, we should find " friendship " up almost at the top. If every person could be a real friend to everyone else, if every nation could be friendly to every other nation, what a fine old world we would have.

I want to tell you two stories and I want you to decide which is the best way to make friends and peace.

The first is this. In 1623, when the Pilgrims were getting settled in America, they were having trouble with the Indians. They always had trouble. The Indians said that they had not been paid for their lands and therefore it was not right for white men to come in and take their best hunting grounds.

Matters became worse. One day the Pilgrims heard that the Indians were going to attack. So Miles Standish and his men went to an appointed place. Peckmot and Wituwamot and several other Indian chiefs called at the log house to see them. All went inside. When they were in, the door was barred and Miles Standish sprang at Peckmot and killed him with his own knife. The other Indians were killed. Immediately a man was sent out to tell white men of other settlements to kill any Indian in their power. It was done. The Indians were angry, but they had lost their leaders and did not fight for several years. Then they sprang up and fought again.

Here is the second. It occurred under a tree in Pennsylvania. This was in very early years also. Some Indians were making their way toward a large oak tree. Some white men were coming from the opposite direction. When very near, suddenly the white men threw their guns away. The Indians threw their bows and arrows away.

It was William Penn, the Quaker, who was leader of the whites. Under the oak tree they sat down and formed a circle. William Penn told them that they wished to buy their lands and would not molest any Indian. The chief said in reply that no Quaker would ever be killed. They kept their promise. No Quaker was ever killed by an Indian. You know the Quakers are called " friends." You can see why now, can you not?

Which do you think was the best way to bring peace, that of Miles Standish or that of William Penn? Which is the best way today? Gunboats and cannon that kill, or the friendship way? We hear sometimes about a war with Japan but that is because we are thinking as Miles Standish did. If we thought of Japanese as friendly to us we could never fight them. You do not go out and kill your friends.

The best way to show folks that you are their friend is to go to them and be friendly. I have here the picture of one who is doing that. This is Alice Cary, a friendly woman, surrounded by Japanese children in Osaka, Japan. She is showing a friendship doll — maybe one sent by this church school, we cannot be sure. Alice Cary is being a real friend to these children. She is in a neighborhood house in a factory city like Pittsburgh. The boys and girls have no place to play so they come to this friendly house. Because the number they can take is limited, mothers even give wrong street numbers to get their children into the house. When asked what religion she held a little girl replied, " Same as yours."

The money you give to World Sharing goes direct to such friendly work. When you give a dollar you are giving a dollar's worth of friendliness. Do you want to be a friend? Then do not fail to show it by giving all you can to world-sharing friendliness.

"REEL" BOYS AND GIRLS

For as a man thinketh in his heart, so is he.
PROVERBS 23:7

FOR AS BOYS and girls think in their hearts, so are they. Here are two reels used on fishing rods to wind the line in and let it out. They look much alike but they are very different. This one is likely to snarl the line very quickly. One way of fishing is to throw out what is called a plug. You cast it about fifty to a hundred feet. The reel spins very fast as the line goes out. When the plug strikes the water this reel keeps on turning, and soon the line is snarled. It takes minutes of precious fishing time to unsnarl it. If you are clever enough you can put your thumb on the reel just as the plug strikes the water. That will keep the line from snarling or tangling, but you see, to do that one must stand over this reel with one's thumb all the time.

The other is called a " level winding, anti-back-lash, casting reel." A long name, is it not? Sounds like a girl's name in a story, " Patricia Ann Elizabeth Jones." There is a device on this reel which stops it just as soon as the plug strikes the water. It brakes itself. It stops without outside help. It does not tangle the line. No snarls ever happen on this reel.

You see, one stops itself; the other needs to be stopped. One controls itself; the other needs to be spanked.

Here are two boys. One stamps into the house without cleaning his shoes. He yells through the house, disturbing whatever may be going on, kicks the furniture about or scratches it. He snarls the household. Some-one has to put a thumb on him because he has not learned to stop himself.

The other boy remembers he is coming into a home where folks live, so he cleans his shoes and watches out for the furniture. No back-lash to him. He is a different sort of reel-boy. Anti-back-lash is he. No tangling or snarling; he controls himself.

I know a girl who sometimes has a desire to tease or strike her sister. Otherwise she is usually a sweet little girl. She is like this first reel: failing to control herself, she is often sent to a room to get unsnarled. Her mother always has to put her thumb on her to keep the line from becoming badly tangled. One day in one of these tantrums, or rather afterward when she was getting unsnarled, she thought of an idea. She had heard older people speak of a new leaf at New Year. So she drew a picture of a tree and placed on it a leaf. The next time her reel began to spin and she wanted to strike someone, she actually stopped herself and drew a new leaf on the tree. When I saw the tree, it had three leaves with plenty of room for more. An excellent idea! When that tree is covered with leaves, she will not be so likely to get snarled up and have to unwind in a dark room. She will be a level-winding, anti-back-lash casting reel-girl.

Just as we learn to control ourselves do we become good citizens. And when we have learned to control ourselves in all things, we are genuine; we have character, strength, goodness; we are easy to live with. Let us begin today to add new leaves to our trees, and see what beautiful trees our lives will become.

ARE YOU A JELLY FISH?

*And when Daniel knew that the writing was
signed, he went into his house, and he kneeled
upon his knees three times a day, and prayed, and
gave thanks before his God, as he did aforetime.*
DANIEL 6:10

A hydromeduson or some similar colenterate.
STANDARD DICTIONARY

DO YOU KNOW what a jelly fish is? It is a queer sort of
fish which looks very like an inverted saucer or umbrella. It may be very small or a yard across. It is
whitish, jelly-like, almost wholly composed of water,
without the backbone or nerves that other animals have.
By contracting the umbrella, it manages to swim a little,
but mostly it drifts with the surface currents. The dictionary says that jelly fish are numerous in summer, rare
in cold weather, and on stormy days descend to quiet
levels.

The story is told of three boys who passed a school
when class was in session. One boy was smaller than
the others. In front of the building a large boy said,
" Jimmie, throw this snowball against the door."

" I'm afraid," said Jimmie.

" Aw! don't be a 'fraid-cat. No one will know who
threw it. Go ahead, throw! "

" I don't think I should," answered Jimmie, but he
threw the ball.

By the time the ball hit the door the larger boys were

143

out of sight and Jimmie had to face the teacher alone. Of course he was punished. He should have been. What was he? His backbone was missing.

Did you ever hear a snobbish little girl say something very mean about some other girl, something you knew was not true? Did you have enough courage to say, " I beg pardon, but I happen to know that that is not quite true "? If you did not, you were a jelly fish, which mostly drifts with the surface currents, having no will power of its own.

There are other kinds of jelly fish. Here are a boy and girl who cannot make up their minds about anything. You ask, " Are you going to join the church attendance class? " The jelly fish answers, " I don't know. I'll see." It waits till it sees which way the gang is flowing and then drifts with the surface currents. You ask another, " Will you come over and play with me? " The answer is, " Maybe I will." Maybe it will and maybe it won't. It depends upon which way the wind is blowing at the time.

Sometimes jelly fish are a yard across, and sometimes small jelly fish grow to be big fish. But a large jelly fish does not have a bit more backbone than a small one. It still dawdles and hesitates. It still follows the gang. It continues to drift with surface currents.

" Numerous in summer, rare in cold weather, on stormy days descend to quiet levels." I thought of some members of this class when I read that. Lots of them in summer, few in cold weather, and on stormy days they go down deeper where it is quiet. How rare they are in cold weather, and how numerous when the sun is shining. When a storm comes on Sunday mornings, watch them: they descend to quiet levels. That is to say, when courage, will power, or nerve are required,

144

they simply are not here. They are found where things are easier and no backbone is required.

The Daniel of our text was exactly the opposite of these jelly-like fish. When he learned that it might mean death to pray as he had done before, he knelt down and prayed. He was more like a sword fish, was he not? He knew what he should do and he had the stiff backbone to do it.

Why be a jelly fish?

ACKNOWLEDGMENTS

Acknowledgment is gratefully made to the following publishers and authors for permission to use stories, verse and other material.

To *New York Herald Tribune Magazine* and the author, Orland K. Armstrong, for the story included in the talk " Roosevelt — the Gentleman."

To the American Book Company, publishers of McGuffey's readers, for the stanza " Lazy Ned " and stories: the boys and the snowball, Gretchen and the gold piece, and the boy chopping wood, which the author remembered from childhood days in a district school.

To Mildred Smith for the story of " Nut Grass or Cotton Plant."

To the *American Magazine* for the story " How a Dog Risked His Life."

To the MacMillan Company, publishers, for the verse by Lewis Carroll from *Alice Through the Looking Glass.*

To the Friendship Press, Missionary Education Movement of the United States and Canada, for " The Story of a Friend," by Margaret E. Burton in the book *Comrades in Service,* from which the facts included in the talk by that title were taken.

To the Abingdon Press for the facts from F. W. Boreham's book *A Handful of Stars,* copyright 1922, upon which the talk " Tell Us a Story About Cannibals " is based.

To Charles Scribner's Sons, publishers, for " The Duel " by Eugene Field.